How I Made

Big Money

Trading Stock Options

By

Carl Allen Schoner

Published by Carl Allen Schoner

CAS Associates
P.O. Box 4462
Diamond Bar, CA 91765

© 2014 by Carl Allen Schoner

All original artwork by Carl Allen Schoner

www.lulu.com/spotlight/carl_schoner
cschoner@netzero.com
dreampsycles@yahoo.com

ISBN: 978-1-304-78057-7

Printed in the United States of America

Second Edition printing January, 2014

7901524-31

I am going to dedicate this book to *nobody,* because *nobody* offered me advice and/or encouragement to take a leap into trading stock options. In fact, almost everyone with whom I discussed this idea told me I was crazy. I'm not sure if they meant I was crazy because I wanted to jump into trading stock options, or if they meant I was crazy in the more general sense of the word. Perhaps time will tell. But the truth is, if I had listened only to the advice of those around me, I would never have gotten out of bed. Instead, I took a giant leap and I have gained quite handsomely from that decision. I have *lost* some money as well, but it goes without saying that there is no gain without at least *some* pain in the form of risk. But the most valuable gain I have realized is in my expanding knowledge of how I *can* make big money in the stock market by making relatively painless decisions! With this new knowledge I felt empowered enough to promote myself to "CEO" of my own financial empire, modest as it may be. I no longer need to rely on others to make my investment decisions for me. This new and *powerful* knowledge can never be taken away, and I can use it over and over again in the future to further improve the bottom line of my own growing portfolio. Thanks to me for not relying solely on the advice of my friends!

TABLE OF CONTENTS

Introduction

I have been actively trading stocks for about 15 years, and in all of those years I have never been more excited about trading than I am today. I say this just one year after the greatest financial meltdown the world has suffered through since the last Great Depression. Not only was the U.S. stock market decimated, but the entire global economy was thrust into a spiral of unprecedented decline. In that meltdown I saw the values of my self-managed IRAs and passively managed 403b portfolios literally cut in half, although the reduction in my IRAs was purely a loss of profit, while the huge reduction in my 403b portfolio cut deeply into principle.

Now, on the heels of what looks like the most amazing stock *rally* in the last 25 years, my personal portfolio has regained all of its losses and is once again well into the black, while my passively managed 403b portfolio is still about 12% under water. I attribute the better performance of my personally managed portfolio to the fact that I have assumed a more active role in managing my money there, aggressively seeking out new opportunities on the one hand while cautiously avoiding undue risks on the other. In short, I am now a moderately conservative investor who is not afraid to take calculated risks.

At one point during the meltdown I retreated entirely into cash in my personal portfolio, while my 403b was 100% in stock and continued to bleed profusely. So like everyone else who got burnt in the meltdown, I wasn't eager to jump back into stock positions, even when the market ultimately seemed to be turning around. Instead I kept much of my portfolio in the safer havens of liquid cash and bonds while I explored other investment strategies and waited for the market to stabilize.

What I learned during this period completely changed the way I think about investing. When I first started investing in stocks, I was of the belief that you should "buy and hold." This strategy certainly did not work for most people who simply bought stocks between 1998 and 2008 only to see their share values fall below 1998 levels at the end of that very long decade. I, however, rapidly evolved into a more moderately aggressive yet still conservative trader about halfway through that period. My strategy was to actively trade, looking to buy solid equities with strong upside potential and using stop-limit orders to sell them to protect my gains once they exceeded a 25% return, with the stop-limit price locking me in at about 20%. This worked well with some of my picks, and my annualized rate of return often far exceeded 50% on the best of them. But I didn't always make the right calls, so my strategy also left me holding a lot of dogs that were either too slow to move on the upside, moved sideways over extended periods of time, or even declined in value while others were appreciating. I knew that there must be a way to increase my return on all of these positions without increasing my overall risk, and it finally occurred to me that I do indeed have many other options that will serve this purpose, and those options are *stock options*.

I had never before considered trading stock options as a strategy that I would employ in my own portfolio. I assumed that trading options was an extremely risky, complex strategy that was best left to professionals who, I imagined, committed vast amounts of money to buy and sell risky options in highly leveraged margin accounts. I knew many inexperienced day-traders who lost their shirts buying and selling on margin, and I had no intention of joining their ranks. And every time I attempted to read a book about trading stock options, I dozed off to sleep because the material was either far too dry, or the presentation much too complicated for me to understand.

I thought there must be an easier way, and I ultimately decided that the best way to learn about options was to simply leap in and apply for *limited trading privileges* in my already open brokerage account. So that is what I did, and that decision proved to be one of the best educational experiences of my life!

In the application process I discovered that at my brokerage (Schwab) there are four levels of privileges one could apply for in an options account. The first (level 0) is the most basic, while the fourth level is reserved only for expert traders with all of the appropriate resources to trade in heavily margined accounts. I applied for and was soon granted level 0 access. Shortly after that I made my very first option trade, not so much on an educated guess as it was on a pure whim to simply discover how the transaction would eventually pan out. What I learned was astonishing, and it completely changed the way I think about making money by trading stocks.

There are many books in print on trading stock options, but most of them (even those written for "dummies") seem to have been written by people with the goal of impressing you with their mastery of complex mathematical formulas, rather than discussing the simple essentials. In this little book I will teach you only what I have personally learned and practiced. I will do this in as straight forward a manner as possible, avoiding all of the technical talk and instead giving you the basics of trading options at the level at which I am approved to trade. I will use actual case studies of my first 40 option trades, and provide all of the details of how I got into these positions, and out of them, and how this impacted my bottom line.

I am confident that by the time you are through reading this little book you will know as much about the practical application of options trading as I did at the time I wrote it; perhaps even more. You will also know how well my first 40 transactions panned out, and this should demonstrate how safe or dangerous trading options can be! In the end, I am confident that you will also be as excited as I am about the rich financial rewards that stock options can provide while at the same time reducing your exposure to the normal risks associated with day trading. So let's get started and make some money!

Section 1 - Why Trade Options?

Why should anyone engage in trading options? If you pose this question to the average person that you encounter on "Main Street" their response will likely be a lengthy string of reasons why you should *never* trade in stock options. "Only experts on Wall Street trade options, and they only trade for their rich clients!" is a likely reply. "It's far too complicated a process; you can never understand it!" is a common objection. "It is much too dangerous and risky – you could get wiped out!" is a likely warning. "It's a tax nightmare!" is yet another. "Trading options is for fools who are determined to loose their money!" is another common admonition. Even the renowned investment guru Peter Lynch (born on my birthday in 1944) has stated his belief that trading options is far too risky and complicated a process, and has advocated this position by advising investors to *stay away from options altogether* and instead to simply "invest in what you know." But you might also encounter that erudite *someone* who *does* know something about options and who might offer you a whole slew of reasons why you should consider trading in this market (and we will discuss most of those reasons in this book). And the single most compelling reason that he will offer is simple: Trading options empowers you with ways to *make more money*!

The truth is that trading options does not have to be anywhere near as complicated as most of what is written on the subject will lead you to believe. You do not have to be a genius or financial guru or rocket scientist to understand how to make money with options. Anyone can succeed by simply sticking to some very basic principles that I will illustrate completely in the pages of this booklet. And you do not have to comprehend all of the different options strategies in order to begin making money. In fact, once you understand just one strategy and its underlying principle clearly, then you can use that knowledge over and over again to make more money on all your trades.

And there are many ways in which trading options can enhance your portfolio. First, I will show you how you can assume control over an underlying stock at a fraction of what it would cost to purchase it outright. Then, I will show you how to trade stock options with your primary goal being to generate additional, *substantial* income from stocks that you currently own, and you will be surprised at how much you can generate! I will also show you how to use options to *leverage the risk* of either buying or selling shares of an underlying stock. I will show you how you can purchase stocks that you really want at well below the current asking price, and how to sell stocks that you really want to get rid of at well above the current bid price.

Finally, I will show you how to use stock options as both *leverage against risk and insurance against loss.* I will cover all of this with actual case studies of my own options trades including spreadsheets that support and illustrate the principles I will present in these sections.

Trading options gives you the ability to increase your profits in many more ways than I can possibly explain in an introductory booklet such as this one. But I will teach you all that I have learned, and share with you my simple strategies for making money with options. No longer do you have to wait passively for your stock positions to appreciate or decline, or watch in vain as buying opportunities slip away. With options it is always possible to generate big income whether the market is moving upwards, downwards, or sideways!

In this booklet I will show you how to do all of these things. But I am going to take a unique approach – one that you are not likely to find in the typical book on trading options. You see, most of these books *are* written by egg-headed PhD's and the like who love to impress you with their math acumen by littering their pages with complex arcane formulas that even they do not fully understand. I will do none of that. Instead, I am writing this little booklet for the benefit of the complete novice when it comes to options. What I write is what I – as a novice myself – have learned along the way. In this learning process I quickly assumed a number of positions with both calls and puts, and in my first few trades I generated an income of $4,000 without buying or selling *any* stock! I was a little nervous at first. I suppose it is my nature to be that way. After all, I was a *complete novice* when I placed my very first options trade, and I certainly didn't want to lose any money! And yet I made that plunge, and I stuck with my personal resolve to learn, and now I find that my worries were all unfounded. Not only have I *not lost a single dime* trading options, but I am actually making big money by doing so! And I am much more comfortable in the stock positions that I currently hold, knowing that I can still profit on them no matter what direction the market is headed.

Will I manage to do even better in my future trades? Time will tell, and this book, in a way, will be my report card. Rather than preach to you about the potential profits to be gained by trading options, I will instead dive head first into trading real options on real stocks, making all of my trades while you stand over my shoulder and scrutinize my strategy. I will explain all of my decisions in detail as I write this book so that you as my partner can judge for yourself how well I do in the end. And let there be no doubt about this: If I can be successful trading options, so can you!

Section 2 - What is a Stock Option?

So what exactly is a stock option? Well, succinctly stated a stock option is simply the right to buy or sell a position in some equity at some fixed price at some future point in time. The option could represent a specific number of shares of stock, commodities, treasuries, or even ETF's - Exchange Traded Funds. The truth is that for every financial market on earth, there is probably a secondary market surrounding it in which options are bought and sold.

There is a wealth of information in print about trading stock options, but you do not have to buy every book on the subject and study them laboriously in order to succeed. In fact, the *Options Industry Council* provides a wealth of free information that you can access via classroom instruction, online study, or even have shipped to your home.

But I think the quickest way to learn about the options market is to research it online. Just do a Google search for "Trading Options" and you will get almost a million hits! You can also go to almost any online brokerage, do a search for a specific stock ticker symbol, and somewhere on the screen you will see a tab or link labeled "Options." When you click on that you will be taken to another screen that will show a number of options, each with a cryptic-looking ticker symbol that may or may not bear any resemblance to the underlying stock that the option represents. Consider the following list of MAR 10 options for PAY (Verifone Corporation):

CALL OPTIONS						Expire at close Fri, Mar 19, 201	
Strike	Symbol	Last	Chg	Bid	Ask	Vol	Open Int
15.00	PAY100320C00015000	4.80	0.00	7.60	8.40	0	10
17.50	PAY100320C00017500	5.72	0.00	5.30	5.90	1	51
20.00	PAY100320C00020000	3.10	↑0.20	2.95	3.40	2	898
22.50	PAY100320C00022500	0.90	↑0.30	0.65	0.80	2	1,549
25.00	PAY100320C00025000	0.15	0.00	N/A	0.10	441	541

PUT OPTIONS						Expire at close Fri, Mar 19, 2010	
Strike	Symbol	Last	Chg	Bid	Ask	Vol	Open Int
17.50	PAY100320P00017500	0.05	0.00	N/A	0.10	24	1,268
20.00	PAY100320P00020000	0.15	0.00	N/A	0.10	0	452
22.50	PAY100320P00022500	0.45	0.00	0.10	0.30	25	75
25.00	PAY100320P00025000	2.25	0.00	1.70	2.35	40	29

You can see that these options are divided into two distinct groups, the top group being "CALL" options while the bottom group represents "PUT" options. A "call" is simply an option to *buy* a number of shares of the underlying equity at some point in the future at a price that is determined today. A "put" is just the opposite; it is the right to *sell* a certain number of shares of the underlying equity at some point in the future at a price that is determined today.

Next to the option strike price column will be a symbol description that tells you a little more about the option. It will be a label that reads a little like this: "PAY100320C00015000" and as you look above and below this label you will notice that the options listed above and below will have similar labels but with different numbers displayed within them. "PAY100320" means that the option is good through March 20th of 2010 (almost all options are good through the third Friday of the month identified in their label). The "C" or "P" in the label stand for "call" or "put", and the 1500 numeric value in the label is the $15 "*strike price*" of the option.

Assume the label "XYZ100116C00007500." This is a call that gives the purchaser the right - *but not the obligation* - to *buy* a fixed number of shares of "XYZ" corporation for $7.50 per share any time between now and Jan 16, 2010. If the option is a *put* and you buy it, then you will have purchased the right to *sell* a fixed number of "XYZ" corporation shares for $7.50 any time between now and Jan 16, 2010. Whether or not you choose to exercise the option will be dependent on whether the price of the underlying stock of XYZ Corporation is above or below the *strike price* on or before the expiration date. In the case of a long call, if the underlying stock had risen to $15 per share, you would exercise your option to buy them at $7.50, immediately sell them for $15, and make an admirable 100% return on your investment. If the option you purchased was instead a *put* and the price of the underlying share had *dropped* to $3.50, you could purchase the shares on the open market at $3.50 and immediately exercise your option to sell them at

$7.50, again, making a respectable 100% return on your investment. I will explain this in greater detail with more examples a little later, but for now the basic concept should be quite clear. *When you buy a call, you buy the right - but not the obligation - to buy a fixed number of shares* of a stock at a specified price any time before the expiration date of the option. *When you buy a put, you are buying the right - but not the obligation - to sell a fixed number of shares* at a specified price any time before the expiration date of the option. Whether or not you do this will be *wholly dependent* on whether the underlying stock price is above or below the strike price of the option on or before the expiration date.

Before you can decide if an option is a good deal or not you will need to know a lot more, of course, not only about the underlying stock, but also many other details of the option such as bid and ask prices, open interest, and volatility. Usually, if you click on the ticker symbol for an option it is possible to drill down for a more detailed look as shown below:

PAY Oct 2010 17.500 call (OPR: PAY101016C00017500)

Last Trade:	3.50	Day's Range:	3.50 - 3.50
Trade Time:	Feb 24	Contract Range:	3.50 - 3.50
Change:	0.00 (0.00%)	Volume:	0
Prev Close:	3.50	Open Interest:	10
Open:	N/A	Strike:	17.50
Bid:	6.00	Expire Date:	15-Oct-10
Ask:	6.80		

In these drilled-down views you will usually find a few columns of numbers that represent the last price paid for the option, the current bid price, the current asking price, the total volume of contracts sold on that day, perhaps the total size (in number of contracts) of the current bid and ask prices, and finally a number labeled "Open Interest." When you are done reading this booklet you will understand what all of these numbers represent, but for now let's focus on the basics.

The "Last" price is the price paid for the very last contract that traded hands. Say for example that the last price paid for a JAN 2010 call to purchase 100 shares of XYZ Corporation at $7.50 per share is .35 cents. No matter whether you are buying or selling options, an option trade is a contract and in most cases a single contract represents 100 shares of the underlying stock. The .35 cents represents the price paid for the right to trade 1 share, but since a contract usually represents 100 shares, then a single contract will cost .35 x 100 = $35.00, plus brokerage commissions. At Charles Schwab the brokerage commission for options is $8.95 + .75 for the first contract, plus .75 for each additional contract. So the total amount needed to purchase this contract will be $35.00 + $8.95 + .75, for a grand total of $44.70. If you wanted to purchase 10 contracts instead, your total cost would be $35.00 + $8.95 + .75 + an additional .75 for each of the other 9 contracts, for a total of $366.45 (these figures would be credited to your account if you were the seller, rather than the buyer of these contracts). The total number of shares that a contract represents *can* be different; for example, if there was a stock split after the issue of the option, but I will not go into these details here since this is the exception rather than the rule. For the purpose of this discussion, let's assume that a contract represents 100 shares.

You will also notice as you examine these options that the last price paid for an option varies a great deal depending on two other very significant variables, one of those being the expiration date, and the other being the strike price. You will notice that in the case of a call, the last price paid will be much higher when the underlying stock price is higher than the strike price of the option, and lower if the underlying share is currently lower than the strike price. With puts, you will notice that the lower the current underlying stock price is relative to the strike price, the higher the price of the option will be. And with both puts and calls, the further off the expiration date, the more variance there will be between the asking price of the options and that of their underlying stocks. For now don't get too hung up on these prices. It will all become clearer to you as you learn more about how options are traded. Just understand that the prices fluctuate just like stocks do, but often with much greater volatility, and this volatility can produce huge gains!

The reason for these volatile price variations is simple enough to understand. First, if you own an option that gives you the right to buy 100 shares of XYZ at $7 per share at a time when its market price is $10 per share, then your option has an *intrinsic* value of $3. The intrinsic value, in very simple terms, is a measure of how much the option is "in the money." An option to buy stock at $7 per share when the market price is $10 per share is $3 *in the money*, or "ITM."

The absolute *worth* of an option will never be less than its *intrinsic value*, and the holder of an "ITM" option really has two choices as to how to cash in on his profit. The first choice might be to exercise the option to buy the stock at $7 per share and immediately sell it for $10 per share on the open market (the brokerage and Options Clearing Corporation will handle the details). His second choice might be to sell the option itself for at least $3 x 100 (the number of shares represented by the contract). In both cases he would end up $300 in his pocket (minus the cost of purchasing the option). That is right! When you purchase an option, you can always sell it anytime before its expiration date on the options market and, just like stocks, the price for options changes in real time as the options are bought and sold. So when you own an option, you have the chance of making money by either exercising the option to buy and sell the underlying stock for a profit, or you might simply *sell the option.* The differences offer a profound insight into the value of trading options. Assume that we are talking 10 call contracts instead of 1, representing 1000 shares instead of 100, and that these contracts were purchased OTM (out of the money), with a strike price of $7 when the stock was selling at $4 per share. The total price to purchase these 10 contracts might have been .05 x 100 = $5 (per contract) x 10 contracts = $50, plus commission ($8.95 + .75 x 10 = $16.45). So the total cost to purchase these contracts might have been $66.45.

To purchase the stock outright at that time would have required $4000.00 + commissions, and that is a considerable amount of money to put at risk! Unless you are absolutely sure about the direction that the stock will move, you are taking a big chance by investing $4000 in a stock when you could gain identical control over the stock for only $66.45!

Assume the stock goes to $10. Our investor could have purchased 10 call contracts for $66.45 and sold them for $3000 ($3.00 x 100 x 10) for an astounding 4400% gain. If he had purchased the stock for $4,000 and then sold it for $10,000 he would have a $6000 profit. This is a larger sum of money but a much more modest 150% gain. Imagine if he had put the $4,000 in options instead, and that $4,000 produced a 4400% return - $60,000! This is but one of the advantages of options!

The most basic options trade it to take a long position by purchasing either a call or a put to open a position, giving you the right – but not the obligation – to buy or sell shares. If you sell the option later, you "sell to close" that position and hopefully make a profit, or at least regain the premium you paid. This is a very important point, but for now just remember that when you buy a call or a put to open a position, you can sell it later to close that position if you choose.

My very first two option trades were calls I bought to open two separate positions on AIG stock, which was highly volatile at the time. You have already learned a very valuable lesson, and that is that the price of an option can be much more volatile than the price of its underlying stock. My next two trades were to sell these calls to close my positions when the price of AIG stock rose quite unexpectedly by 24% in one day, and the value of my options rose by over 440%!

And now you must be asking yourself, "If there is so much money to be made trading call options, why bother with trading stocks at all? Why not just buy and sell call options?

Well, it turns out that there is one very good reason why you don't want to do that. The ugly truth is that most *long* call options simply expire! That is to say, after you *purchase* one, there is a very good chance that if you do nothing else in the future it will simply expire worthless! If the movement of the underlying stock is not fast enough and in the right direction, you will neither be able to exercise the option or sell it at a profit, and you will then lose your investment altogether!

What makes *only* buying calls so risky is that one other, all important variable of all options. *Time*, in the form of the *expiration date* approaches all too quickly, first diminishing and finally erasing the value of options approaching expiration. As the *time value* of an option diminishes and the strike price seems unattainable, open interest wanes, bidders disappear, and the call expires with the buyer losing all premiums paid.

Worse things could have happened, of course. You might have bought $7,000 of XYZ Corporation stock only to watch its market value fall to $3000 in the same amount of time, and in this case your paper loss, at least, would be much greater than your $66.45 premium loss. On the other hand, it would not be a 100% loss, and the stock might also rise if you held it long enough. But buying a call and holding it until expiration is not the only way to trade options, and in fact, this approach is really one of the riskiest ways to invest in options if done alone. Fortunately, there is more than one way to skin a cat when you are trading options!

So now you know that you can buy and sell options to open and close a position in the underlying stock. An option bought to open a position is a contract, and it gives you the right - *but not the obligation* - to buy or sell shares of a specific stock at a specific price on or before some specified date in the future. Knowing this, you now know a lot about options!

But what if the stock does hit the strike price and you decide to exercise the option? Isn't someone obligated to either buy shares from you, or sell their shares to you if you chose to exercise the option? The answer is "Yes," and that person is the one who *wrote the option*. When you write an option you *sell it to open* a position. For example, you might sell a call option that gives the buyer the right - but not the obligation - to buy 100 shares of XYZ Corporation *from you* at $10 per share anytime between now and the expiration date of the contract. As the *writer* of the contract, you pocket the premium paid for the contract the moment you sell it, but you are also *obligated* to sell the specified number of shares *at the strike price* to the contract holder if he or she elects to exercise the option to buy them. If you had sold a put, then you would be obligated to purchase those shares at the strike price. Why would you want to do this? Well, first of all - you pocket the premium paid for the contract! It is immediate income and often times substantial income. Second - and this is the *really* important point - almost

90 percent of the time, the option you sold will simply expire! You will not have to buy or sell shares in XYZ Corporation, and the premium you pocketed for the sale of the contract will have been earning good income either in a risk free investment, or through the purchase of additional options! You must be prepared to either buy or deliver shares if the contract holder chooses to exercise, but if you picked your strike price properly, you will be happy to do so!

So these are the basic points to remember: You *buy calls and puts to open a position giving you the right, but not the obligation to exercise the option.* You can later sell these options to close your position and possible make a profit on the sale. You can also exercise the option to make a profit, or you could let the option expire and lose the premium you paid.

You can also write a contract, which means you *sell a put or a call to open a position.* As a writer, you are *obligated* to either sell or purchase shares of the stock if the holder of the contract decides to exercise that option, but you can buy the option back to *close* a position anytime before the expiration date if you choose to do so. By doing this you will return much of the premium you paid, and perhaps even pay more resulting in a net loss to get out of the position, but sometimes it will be worth it to do so. You will see why when we discuss VALE.

So option traders buy to open and sell to close, while option writers sell to open, and buy to close. When I first began trading options my belief was that it was better to spend a few dollars buying calls to open with the hope that the underlying stock would appreciate greatly, allowing me to either sell the option for a small profit or exercise it for a bigger profit. I soon realized, though, that while this was a valid strategy in some cases, I could make much more money by *writing calls* to sell stock that I currently owned at a healthy profit, or *writing puts* to purchase stocks that I wished to buy at far out of the money prices. For example, if I wished I had bought XYZ when it traded at $50 per share, and it was now trading at $75 per share, I could write (*sell to open*) a put option *that would obligate me to purchase 100 shares of XYZ at $50* per share if the buyer exercised the option. In exchange, I would pocket the premium the buyer paid for this option. Since this put would most likely expire without being exercised I would simply keep a healthy premium, and I could write contract after contract, collecting the premiums this way until someone actually sold me XYZ at $50 per share. But all of those premiums collected would reduce the actual price I paid for XYZ to well below $50 per share! In effect, by writing these contracts, I will be getting paid while I wait for XYZ stock to drop down to the price I am willing to pay, and the premiums I receive will reduce the effective price even further!

Now it is true that the further out of the money a put option contact is, the lower the premium you will collect for it. But if you know what your limits are, then selling contracts essentially generates a free and almost constant income stream. You are getting paid right now to either buy or sell a stock that you really want to buy or sell anyway at some point in the future - at the price you choose. And if you change your mind about this position you can always buy back your option to close out the position and remove your obligation – oftentimes at a profit! That flexibility is the real power of trading options!

Section 3 – Option Risks

There is truth to the argument that trading options is laden with risks, but then again, any investment involves risk. A savvy investor will manage this risk to good advantage, and through the use of options it is possible to reduce the risk of investing to well below the risk of investing in equities alone. I have already demonstrated this with the example of writing (selling) a put contract to purchase XYZ at $50 per share when it is currently selling for $75 per share. The premiums earned will substantially reduce your risk exposure to the stock should you actually purchase it at $50 per share later.

But there are risks involved with option trading that you must fully understand before engaging in any trade. The major risks - limited to the extent of options trading that I will discuss in this book - are detailed below. There are even greater risks for investors and speculators who venture beyond the trading strategies that I will discuss in this book, but for openers, these are the most important risks for you to understand.

When you buy a CALL option, it will *probably* expire worthless. Most call options do. When you buy a call, you are buying a *long* position with the belief that the underlying stock

28

will rise in price to a point high enough over the strike price to allow you to exercise the option and make a healthy profit after deducting the cost of buying the option. Generally, the lower strike price will demand a higher premium. If XYZ Corp is selling at $50 per share and you want to purchase a call to buy it at $49 per share, that option will cost you at least $1 per share. Also, the further away the expiration date, the higher the premium; *this is time value.* Calls can be quite expensive. In this example, if the stock subsequently rises to $52 per share you might be able to make a profit after commissions, but then again, you might not.

Likewise, when you buy a put option it will *probably* also expire worthless. When you buy a long put you are taking a *bearish position* on the underlying stock, meaning that you believe the stock will go down. There are two kinds of people who do this. The first is someone who already owns the stock, does not really want to sell it, but wishes to protect against a sudden and perhaps permanent downturn in the value of those shares. He will purchase an option to sell the stock at some specified strike price, really hoping that the stock will not fall, but reserving the option to sell it at that price should he need to. You can think of this strategy as similar to purchasing a term insurance policy on the stock. The difference between this and simply setting a stop-limit order on the stock is that with a stop-limit order, the stock will definitely be sold when it hits the stop price. The option holder can sell the stock when it falls below the strike price any time before the option expires. But he also has the option to sell the put to close the position at a possible gain. If the stock does not go down the option will expire worthless, and the investor will lose the premium, but the option will have served its purpose of insuring the stock. Still, if you really believe that a stock price is going to tank, why not sell it now rather than *buying the right to sell it later*?

The second kind of investor who purchases a put will buy the option without owning the stock. They might buy an option to sell XYZ at $10 per share when it is currently selling at $10. Their hope is that the stock would drop to say, $5 per share, at which point they would buy it at $5, and immediately sell it at $10, making a 100% profit. Sometimes this happens, but more often it does not and the option expires worthless.

When you purchase an option to open a position, your maximum loss is limited to the premium you paid. When you purchase a call your potential gain is unlimited, going as high as the value of the underlying stock might rise. When you purchase a put your potential gain is limited to the difference between the strike and stock prices times the number of shares that the contract represents minus the premium paid.

You expose yourself to potentially much greater risks when you sell options to *open a position,* as this makes you the *writer* of the contract. When you sell a call to open a position you are obligating yourself to deliver shares of a given stock at a specified price at some point in the future. If you sell such a contract and you do not own the shares, this is called a *naked call* - the riskiest of all option positions. Assume the contract is for you to deliver 1000 shares of XYZ at $10 in April. In late March XYZ makes a major announcement that causes its shares to rise to $100 in just a few days. The contract holder elects to exercise it, meaning you must now purchase 1000 shares of XYZ at $100 per share ($100,000) and sell them to the holder for $10 per share ($10,000). You just lost $90,000! When you sell a naked call, your potential loses are unlimited!

When you write a put contract, your are obligating yourself to purchase a stock at a specified price at some point in the future, and you must be sure that you have sufficient cash on hand to make the purchase. If you don't, you will have sold a *naked put.* Your exposure is limited to the amount of money required to make the purchase minus the premium earned, but this can be quite damaging if the market moves unexpectedly in the wrong direction and your broker is forced to sell off some of your most coveted holdings to satisfy your margin obligation if you do not have cash on hand.

To minimize these risks in my accounts I intend to follow a simple strategy as I wade into options. I will buy calls on stocks that suffer a major meltdown in price as a result of what I call speculator over-reaction to some news event that shouldn't fundamentally alter the value of the stock. Usually these stocks will recover dramatically shortly after such a meltdown, so there is good potential to make money either on the sale of the call later, or by exercising the option later.

I do not intend to buy puts to open as part of a strategy to preserve gains in stocks I own. I would rather set stop-limit orders, or perhaps sell the stock outright at the higher price. I will tell you why in a little later.

Knowing what I do at this writing, I will only sell calls to open on stocks that I really want to sell and only at a price that I am willing to sell them for. Generally, if a stock I own has gained 25% or more in less than a year and I feel that there is little more opportunity for a big move on the upside, I will write out of the money calls to sell this stock at some price that improves on this 25% return, but does not reduce it.

I will only sell puts on stocks that I really, really want to own, and only at the price that I really want to pay for them. I will generally write out of the money puts for a strike price at

10-20% less than market. I am fortunate in that my brokerage automatically places "on hold" any capital that is required to cover my puts sold to open and will not allow me to write a put requiring more cash than I have in my account. This is one of the trading restrictions placed in my Level 1, limited privilege account. Otherwise, I would run the real risk of overextended myself, and this is the *greatest risk* that options traders face.

Another subtle risk has its roots in greed. It is easy for novice options traders - especially those who write contracts - to become a little over exuberant in their quest for free money. It seems far too easy to generate money by simply writing out of the money contracts with the hope that they will never be exercised and you can simply pocket the premiums without consequence. So you might find yourself writing contracts to purchase stocks that you would never consider purchasing otherwise, or selling stocks that you really do not want to sell.

Another less obvious risk is one of obsession. Trading options is in many ways like gambling. There are elements of skill and chance involved that greatly elevate one's sense of excitement over trading in stocks alone. Successfully trading in options also requires a great deal more time and attention than does simply buying and holding stocks. To this extent, trading in options can easily become a full time obsession.

To reduce this risk and the inherent dangers associated with it, it is imperative that traders know what their entry point is (the cost of getting into a position), where their break even point is, and where their exit points are (to close, exercise, or allow the option to expire) for each and every transaction. If you start trading options without understanding this, you could very well lose your shirt! Toward maintaining a clear and objective understanding of my positions I have developed a spreadsheet model that shows my entry point, a possible exit point for closing the option, and finally what the outcome of an exercised option might be. We will examine many of these models in sections that follow. Shown below is my model for a covered call option I sold to open against my Citicorp stock.

Entry point for my sale of a CALL option on Citicorp:

SYMBOL	OPTION	STRIKE	PRICE-O	COMM	OPEN	TYPE
CCH.o	CALL MAR 10	8	0.15	-16.45	133.55	**CSO**

Exit (buy option back at .05 per contract / retain $67.10):

SYMBOL	PRICE-C	PRICE +/-	CLOSE	GAIN	ROI%
CCH.o	-0.05	-66.67	-66.45	67.10	50.24

Exit (exercised at $8 strike, retain $120.55 after commission.)

STK	SYMBOL	EXEC $	TODAY $	$GAIN	%ROI	P-SHR	%+-STK
C	CCH.o	8000	8000	120.55	90.27	0.12	1.51

Section 4 – Opening an Options Account

The first thing I learned about options is that I had to apply to upgrade my brokerage account to an options account before I could begin trading. Even though you might be able to view options on your brokerage account screen, you will not be able to trade until your brokerage approves your application. Doing that will usually involve filling out a questionnaire that asks about your overall investment experience, financial goals, net worth, and other questions along these lines. You will also have to acknowledge that you have read and understand the disclosure documents warning about the risks involved with trading options. This is really a good thing because it will make you think twice about what you getting yourself into.

Before you even think about opening an options trading account I would urge you to visit the Options Industry Council website at www.888options.com. This is an organization that provides a wealth of free information about options in the form of printed material, CD's and DVDs, interactive online training programs and simulators, and even classroom based training - most free of cost. This is a resource you should bookmark now and visit often, as there are many much more sophisticated strategies that might be of interest to you discussed there.

No matter what kind of brokerage account you have, you will probably still have to apply for privileges before you can begin trading options. But before you do apply, there are other considerations that you must make as to what kind of account you want to trade in, and at what level. After you have weighed the pros and cons of these various considerations then you will be ready to set up your account and begin trading.

Probably the first thing you will need to decide is which level of privileges you will want to apply for. I will make this simple for you and tell you to apply for only the most basic level to begin. You can always raise the bar later (I went from level 0 to level 1 in just two weeks). By starting at level 0, you are eliminating the possibility of making any really serious mistakes while you are learning exactly how far you can push the envelope at this level. Better safe than sorry!

While it is possible to trade options without owning stock to being with, this is somewhat risky for the beginner and I would advise against this. That certainly isn't the route that I elected to take! Instead, I set up my options privileges in an account in which I already owned many stocks. I also had some cash set aside in this account, as you should too when you start with options, *whether your intent is to buy or write contracts*. Do not assume for a moment that your cash flow will always be positive! I learned that selling contracts can severely restrict your cash flow if not done properly! But with both stocks and cash on hand, you can immediately trade both covered calls - the most conservative of all investments - and sell covered puts (your cash will "cover" any puts sold to open). Plan on starting small and upping the ante only after your confidence is fully matched by practical knowledge and skills.

Another important decision I had to make was whether to set up my options privileges in a regular brokerage account, a traditional IRA, or a Roth IRA account. While I am sure that many financial advisors would steer you away from trading options in an IRA (you shouldn't gamble with your nest egg!) there are some good reasons for trading in such an account. In a traditional IRA any profits you make will grow tax-free until that time you begin drawing from the account, and at that time they will be taxed as regular income. Of course, you cannot begin to draw these funds until you are at least 59 1/2, but that is true whether or not you trade options within the account.

If you trade options within a Roth IRA, then any of the profits you make will be *tax free forever*. So if you are really good and make (oh, what the heck) *millions* of dollars trading options, then that will be *tax free income – pure profits* - and you will have been a very, very savvy investor indeed!

I learned that if I set up options privileges and traded in a standard brokerage account then I could draw profits from the account at any time I choose, although I would be taxed on my profits. What's more, my profits may be taxed as either short term gains or taxed as long term gains depending on some very complex formulas that factor in the kind of option you traded and how long you owned the underlying shares. This kind of record keeping and tax reporting is not for the feint of heart, so I would recommend that you talk with a tax advisor before trading options in a standard brokerage account.

Your brokerage firm may or may not require that your options account be a marginable account. They may or may not allow you to trade in an IRA. They may require that you maintain a certain amount of money in the account. The only way you will know for sure what qualifications your brokerage will require of you is for you to fill out an application, research them online, or discuss these matters in a phone interview. But no matter what kind of account you set up, it will always be up to you to ensure than any trade you engage in does not leave you open to over-exposure and unanticipated risk. In the end, the risk is all yours, and if you make a mistake, you will pay dearly for it! Like a pit boss in a gambling casino, brokerages are very unforgiving of your mistakes.

Well, all things considered I eventually applied for and received approval to trade options in all three of my brokerage accounts: standard, traditional IRA, and Roth IRA. But after reading the fine print over and over again, I decided to limit my initial trading to my IRA accounts! This is exactly what most financial advisors would advise against, but my reasoning was simple. I wanted to avoid more than anything the tax reporting nightmares and complex formulas involved in calculating taxes in a standard brokerage account. My decision was to start in a tax sheltered account, concentrating only on option basics and not worrying about the tax laws as they pertain to a standard account. I'm glad I did, because I now know that had I executed all of the trades discussed in this book in my standard brokerage account, it would have created a tax nightmare for me in 2009! At the very least I might have had to pay a tax professional many hundreds of dollars to sort it all out for me. Whew! I am glad I dodged that bullet!

My word of advice here is simple: *do not trade options in a standard brokerage account until you have spoken with a qualified tax advisor and understand all of the implications of in that account*! Only after you are fully versed in all of the tax laws should you consider trading in a standard account. All of that aside, once your account is approved and funded, you are ready to begin trading!

Section 5 – Tracking Models

As I alluded to earlier, if you are going to trade stocks and options you must have some method of tracking your transactions, calculating your costs, break even points, returns and such, and otherwise simply measuring your success. I have found that the best tool for doing this is a simple spreadsheet.

Of course, if you are trading stocks you should use a spreadsheet for tracking your transactions, but this is especially true if you are also going to trade options. The model I use is shown below. Since it is too large to fit on one page, I have divided it into two sections. The first section shows the total number of shares purchased and sold, the total amount of dollars invested and returned (sold), the number of days the equity was held, the number of shares held, the position/risk (a negative number here means you have realized a better than 100% return), and finally the market value of the equity.

SYMBOL	SHR_BUY	SHR_SEL	INVESTED	SOLD	DAYS	SHR_HLD	POS/RISK	MARKET
	2958.49	300.00	25858.60	8921.87	10880	2658.49	16936.73	19451.43
AOB.2	450.00	0.00	3390.10	2958.49	300	450.00	6775.68	2155.50
C.2	1006.11	0.00	5060.00	387.10	183	1006.11	4672.90	4537.57
CDII.5	200.00	0.00	300.00	39.55	32	200.00	260.45	316.00
EROC.5	100.00	0.00	386.00	80.30	90	100.00	305.70	531.00
GE.5	302.38	300.00	3900.00	4429.30	81	2.38	-529.30	37.36
MEA.2	500.00	0.00	3150.00	670.48	172	500.00	2479.52	2230.00
VALE*.*	200.00	0.00	5062.50	287.10	150	200.00	4775.40	5524.00
VLO*.5	200.00	0.00	4610.00	69.55	148	200.00	4540.45	4120.00
TOTALS	2958.49	300.00	25858.60	8921.87	144	2658.49	23280.80	19451.43

The second section shown below is a continuation of that above; i.e., the columns that continue to the right. It shows the average price I paid per share, the average price of sold shares, the current quote (price) for the stock, the dollar gain (or loss) of my trades on the equity, the percent gain (or loss), the annualized rate of return (or loss), my profit or loss per share, and how much of this profit or loss is held (a paper loss), or realized.

AVG-BUY	AVG-SEL	PRICE	GAIN-$	%GAIN	YRLY%	SHR	REALIZED HELD	REALIZED
8.74	22.59	7.32	368.51	1.93	4.51	0.00	(193.69)	562.20
7.53	0.00	4.79	(422.30)	(12.46)	(11.51)	(0.94)	(422.30)	0.00
5.03	0.00	4.51	(135.33)	(2.67)	(5.33)	(0.13)	(135.33)	0.00
1.50	0.00	1.58	55.55	18.52	211.21	0.28	55.55	0.00
3.86	0.00	5.31	225.30	58.37	236.71	2.25	225.30	0.00
12.90	14.76	15.72	566.66	14.53	65.88	1.87	4.45	562.20
6.30	0.00	4.46	(249.52)	(7.92)	(16.81)	(0.50)	(249.52)	0.00
25.31	0.00	27.62	748.60	14.79	36.03	3.74	748.60	0.00
23.05	0.00	20.60	(420.45)	(9.12)	(22.57)	(2.10)	(420.45)	0.00
10.69	14.76	10.57	368.51	1.93	4.51	9.25	(193.69)	562.20

You might be yawning at the prospects of keeping such detailed records and tracking models of your transactions, but I assure you this: unless you do the same, you *will* lose money!

The next model is the one I use to analyze any options I am considering in order to help me determine whether they are a good bet for the price I am likely to pay, and how well they fit into my overall portfolio shown in the previous spreadsheet (in fact, the two are closely linked to function as one).

ACCT	STK	OPTION	SYMBOL	STRIKE	PRICE-O	COMM	OPEN	
		OPTIONS OPEN						
2	AOB	PUT JAN 11	ZZDMA	5	1.65	-12.70	812.30	PSO
2	C	CALL MAR 10	CCH.o	8	0.15	-16.45	133.55	CSO
2	C	PUT JAN 10	CMW.X	4	0.27	-16.45	253.55	PSO
2	ICO	PUT MAR 10	ICOOA	5	1.05	-14.20	720.80	PSO
2	MEA	PUT APR 10	MEAPA.o	5	1.37	-12.70	670.48	PSO
5	CDII	CALL MAR 10	CDSCZ.X	2.5	0.25	-10.45	39.55	CSO
5	EROC	CALL APR 10	EAUDA.X	5	0.90	-9.70	80.30	CSO
5	GE	PUT JAN 10	GEWMV	12.5	0.31	-12.70	142.30	PSO
2	VALE	CALL JAN 10	RFPAY.o	27.5	0.65	-10.45	119.55	CSO
5	VALE	PUT DEC 10	RIOXXo	22.5	0.89	-10.45	167.55	PSO
5	SLV	PUT APR 10	SLVPO.X	15	0.90	-10.45	169.55	PSO
5	VLO	CALL JAN 10	VLBAY.x	25	0.40	-10.45	69.55	CSO
5	SLV	PUT JAN 11	XUXMO.x	15	1.60	-10.45	309.55	PSO

Since I can trade options in more than one account, the first column of my spreadsheet is the account number. The second column I reserve for the ticker symbol of the underlying stock, while the third column is the option type. You can see that the first option is a PUT option for AOB stock with an expiration of JAN 11 and a strike price of $5. The ticker for the option is ZZDMA. The "PSO" in the far right column stands for PUT SELL TO OPEN. Since I sold this option for $1.65 per share for 500 shares, I pocketed $812.30! To review, here is the formula for calculating the premium earned on this call:

$1.65 * 100 = $165 * 5 contracts= 825$ - $12.70 commission.

In fact, if you look at the right-most column in the table above you will see that *all* of the options in this spreadsheet represent options that I *sold to open*. Some are (CSO) or calls sold to open, while the others are (PSO) or puts sold to open. In every case the net amount equals a credit to my account, rather than a debit as would be the case were I buying the options instead. The above spreadsheet reveals to me at a glance how much money I pocketed by selling these positions, but it would also show how much I paid to open any positions.

Now in the case of my AOB stock, my previous purchases averaged $7.53 cents a share. It was trading at about $4.70 at the time I sold the put options. My hope was/is that the option will not be exercised, but if it does then I will be happy to buy AOB at $5 per share because that will lower my average price for the stock. I was paid an additional $812 for my promise to buy AOB at a less than market price! What a deal!

The center section of my spreadsheet model shown on the following page shows the effect of closing an option (it too is a continuation of the previous spreadsheet, so picture them as being side by side). If I don't want an option to be exercised against me, I must close that option. For example - my 5 AOB puts sold to open for $1.65 per contract - a net gain of $812. If the price of the option dropped to .10 cents per contract I could buy an identical 5 puts to close my position for a mere $62.70. I would still keep $749.60 of the $812 I pocketed when I sold the contract to open it, but I would be *free of any future obligation* to buy the stock!

	PRICE-C	PRICE +/-	CLOSE	GAIN	ROI%	P-SHR	%+-STK
PSO	-0.10	-93.94	-62.70	749.60	-7.72	1.62	32.49
CSO	-0.08	-46.67	-96.45	37.10	-72.22	0.13	1.67
PSO	-0.20	-25.93	-216.45	37.10	-85.37	0.25	6.34
PSO	-0.01	-99.05	-21.20	699.60	-2.94	1.03	20.59
PSO	-1.10	-19.49	-562.70	107.78	-83.92	0.97	19.40
CSO	-0.25	0.00	-60.45	-20.90	-152.84	1.34	26.82
CSO	-1.00	11.11	-109.70	-29.40	-136.61	0.20	7.91
PSO	-0.20	-35.48	-112.70	29.60	-79.20	0.28	2.28
CSO	-1.71	163.08	-352.45	-232.90	-294.81	0.60	2.17
PSO	-0.51	-42.70	-112.45	55.10	-67.11	0.84	3.72
PSO	-0.85	-5.56	-180.45	-10.90	-106.43	0.85	5.65
CSO	-0.24	-40.00	-58.45	11.10	-84.04	0.35	1.39
PSO	-1.70	6.25	-350.45	-40.90	-113.21	1.55	10.32

The columns show the original option (PSO=Put Sold to Open and CSO=Call Sell to Open). All of these represent options *sold* to generate money in my account. The PRICE-C column represents the contract price to *buy back the option to close the position.* Since I am spending money to close these positions the contract prices are shown as negative values (cash outlay). The "PRICE +/1" column represents what percentage the price of the option has risen or fallen since I opened the position. CLOSE is the amount paid to close the position. If the original option was a *buy to open* (PBO or CBO) then I would instead *sell to close* the position, and in that case the price and close columns would show *positive numbers representing income.* The GAIN column shows how much of my original premium was ultimately retained or lost when closing the position. ROI% represents the percentage of my *original premium* that was retained or lost when the position was closed. AOB shows a negative ROI% of -7.72% because the original

CSO was worth $812, and in closing it only $749.60 was retained. Finally, the two columns on the right side show two other variables that are very important to consider when trading options. These are how much money you earn or lose per share when the transaction is done, and how much this is over or under the strike price of the option.

You now know that there are three possibilities with every option. It can expire worthless to the buyer (but not to the seller, who profits handsomely when an option expires!). It can be closed, which is what the section of spreadsheet shown immediately above demonstrates, or it can be exercised, as the last section of spreadsheet shown below illustrates.

EXEC	OPEN	CLOSE	GROWTH	EXEC $	TODAY $	$GAIN	%ROI
Y	4.5	4.79	6.44	2500	2395	694.30	85.47
Y	4.5	4.51	0.22	8000	4510	3610.55	2703.52
Y	4.5	4.51	0.22	4000	4510	750.55	296.02
Y	4.2	5.22	24.29	3500	3654	861.80	119.56
Y	4.3	4.46	3.72	2500	2230	387.48	57.79
Y	1.75	1.58	-9.71	500	316	210.55	532.36
Y	4.7	5.31	12.98	500	531	36.30	45.21
Y	16	15.72	-1.75	6250	7860	1739.30	1222.28
Y	25	27.62	10.48	5500	5524	82.55	69.05
Y	25	27.62	10.48	4500	5524	1178.55	703.40
Y	17.5	17.48	-0.11	3000	3496	652.55	384.87
Y	19.25	20.6	7.01	5000	4120	936.55	1346.59
Y	17.5	17.48	-0.11	3000	3496	792.55	256.03

This model demonstrates what the effect of exercising my options would be. The first field is a logical indicator that can be set to "Y" or "N". When set to "Y" indicating that the option is exercised, then all of the other fields are calculated based on the known variables contained in the earlier sections of the whole spreadsheet. If the first column is set to "N" then only the GAIN and ROI% columns would be calculated based on whether was closed out or simply expired.

So there you have it! That is the model I use for analyzing and tracking my option trades. I may include all of these formulas later, but chances are you can figure them out yourself. They are all simple math; no complex functions are involved. You might be scratching your head and wondering why I am getting into these details, but trust me, you will fully understand why as we begin looking a little deeper at some of my individual option trades.

While the options shown in the above models are all "open," I also use these models to explore alternative scenarios of opening, closing, and exercising prospective options. I also maintain a spreadsheet that shows only historical trades. In that model each record shows exactly how the option was opened, exercised, or expired. Please note that many of the examples that follow may include more than one contract, but this should be evident based on the cost of a single contract and the total amount I earned or was paid for each position. This will become clear as we explore each of the examples presented.

Section 6 – Buying Puts and Calls to Open

In this section, and the sections that follow, we'll look at all of the option trading that I did while writing this book. Together they will provide a complete illustration of all the principles that I have learned and applied so far. Let's start by examining the first call options I bought to establish a position. Remember that when you buy a call, you are buying the right, but not the obligation to purchase a stock at a fixed price in the future. We will start by looking at my NOV 09 and JAN 10 calls for AIG, as these comprise my very first options trades.

AIG (Buy CALL to Open)

The very first call I bought to open was a NOV 09 call for AIG with a strike price of $2, and given the statistic that 90% of such options expire worthless and I was a beginner, I should have lost my shirt on this one. Instead, I emerged from the dung heap smelling like roses. Let's see how that happened.

Actually, this AIG option transaction is probably the most complicated of all my option trades because it involved a reverse stock split immediately after I purchased the first call. But as a result of that, this example will probably provide you with a much clearer understanding of how option prices and commissions are based on a universal constant called the "standard multiplier." Stick with me and this will become clear to you, and you will see how I made a good profit as I waded into this most treacherous of options scenarios, regardless of the sudden emergence of this unexpected technicality. Imagine, a novice trader deciding to take a gamble against a dangerous Wall Street financial institution on the brink of bankruptcy!

Keep in mind as you read through the following case studies that, when I say I made a "good profit," I am speaking in terms of a profit as a percentage of my original investment. Too many novice traders jump in too quickly hoping to get rich overnight, only to lose everything. Always start with small trades, and only increase your bets as your knowledge grows!

I had already made a nice 32% profit annualized at about 180% on AIG by jumping in and out of the stock while it made wild swings in its near-death gyrations, but I had no position when I first considered buying a call option. I actually had some seller's remorse for getting out of the stock too soon (a common complaint of mine), but I was reluctant to throw too much of my money back into the stock as public anger at AIG increased for its contribution to the global financial meltdown. Share price had fallen into the gutter, selling for about $1.70, yet it was extremely volatile. While I didn't fully understand why this was true, everything I read indicated that volatility was one of the variables that made a stock a good candidate for options trading, so I thought "what the heck?" I decided to throw $27.70 at a November 09 call to purchase 100 shares of AIG at a strike price of $2.00. It would have cost me $175 to purchase the shares that day on the open market.

What happened next astonished me. I think it was the following week when I checked on the price of AIG stock to find it was $25 per share! Imagine my excitement as I did the math on exercising this option immediately, buying 100 shares of AIG at $2.00, and selling them for $25 for a quick $2,300 and 1100% profit! But when I went into my account to exercise the trade, I noticed that the ticker symbol of my option had changed! Originally it was labeled something like AIGAU.o but now it showed up as UZLKU.o in my account. Not only that, but the detailed description of the option changed from "CALL AIG NOV 09 2.00" to "CALL AIG NOV 09 2.00 REP 5 SHRS". When I called my brokerage to inquire about this change, I was told that AIG had exercised a reverse 5/100 split, and that as a result of this for every 100 shares that my contract previously represented, it now represented only 5 shares! Each share of AIG was now *worth* twenty times as much, though, so now AIG was once again trading above $25 per share!

The reason AIG exercised the reverse stock split was a desperate attempt to try to increase the *perceived* value of its shares in the minds of investors, and also to avoid being dropped from trading on the New York Stock Exchange, which typically does not list stocks that trade at less than a dollar. Months earlier, this stock had been trading at more than $70 per share! Volatility is one of the variables you look for when considering stocks you might trade options on, and AIG had plenty of volatility, even if it was now almost all taxpayer owned with little hope of turning a profit in the next decade!

So I was incredibly excited at the thought that I could exercise my option to purchase 100 shares of AIG at $2 and immediately sell them at $25. My broker, however, explained to my dismay that this was not the way it worked. When a stock splits, options associated with it also split, in a sense. That is why the option ticker changed, and why the option label now said "REP 5 SHRS", or "Represents 5 shares."

You will recall that all options trade in contracts that usually represent 100 shares, and for this reason 100 is used as the "standard multiplier" to calculate the cost of buying, selling, or exercising contract. If a contract has a strike price of $2, then the formula for calculating the cost of exercising the contract is calculated as $2.00 x 100 + commission ($12.95 at

Schwab) for a total of $212.95. *So I naturally assumed that my cost to purchase shares when I exercised the option* would be $212.95. However, even though the standard multiplier of 100 is used, the number of shares represented by my contract *after the reverse split* was now only 5; this changed everything!

So while it would now cost me exactly $212.95 to exercise the purchase, I would only receive 5 shares, and could only sell them for $125 (5 x $25), leaving me with an $87.95 loss! Subtract from this amount the original cost of purchasing the option ($27.70) and my loss grows to $115.65! After some quick calculations the broker told me that because of the split my break even point had risen to $50 per share, so in order to exercise this option at a gain the stock would have to rise above $50! What I learned to my total dismay was that my option was essentially *worthless* as a result of the split, *at that point in time.* But I didn't know how to calculate the *time value* of an option, nor did I realize how quickly this value can change.

Well, I still had an awful lot to learn about options! About the same time as this discovery, the price of AIG stock plummeted (nobody really believed it was worth $25 per share) and it dropped all the way down to around $7 per share. As the price of the stock dropped so did the price of many AIG call options, especially those special options that only represented 5 shares and were already deemed worthless. I came across one of these worthless options selling at only .01 per contract so I purchased 10 contracts, for a total cost to me of $26.45 on the whim that maybe, just *maybe* the stock would rise again and I could achieve a break even on my total investment, or even realize a small profit if the price of the stock were to rise. Still, this was only my second call option purchased, and I bought it not so much on the belief that I would make money as I did with an expectation that I would at least learn something more about call options through this small investment.

Besides, I had read an interesting story in an online business blog about some options trader who was taking a huge position with an "*options strangle*" on AIG. Essentially he took both a long call and a long put position on AIG at two different strike prices but identical expiration dates, doing so of course with the expectation that he was going to make a substantially profit on the heels of a big expected change in AIG's stock price – either way! I was impressed with the concept of this "options strangle" and how this position would give the investor unlimited potential gains while limiting his risk to the premiums paid. I didn't really understand the math, but decided that maybe I should just pick up another call option on AIG to keep me invested and involved enough to learn more on the concept and see this drama played out.

Well, about a month later the CEO of AIG made some positive comments (but baloney nonetheless) to the press about the company. Things such as "I believe we can pay off our debt to the U.S. taxpayers early!" and "We might even make some money for our stockholders this year!" and many speculators bought this nonsense! In just one day they drove up the price of AIG stock over 25%! On that same day I realized that the price of my options went up too, and while I quickly sold my first option for $12 and was happy to recoup 50% of my original investment, I sold my second call option to close my position with a net gain of $117 - a small dollar amount but a whopping 442% *gain* in less than two weeks! I can only imagine how much money that daring trader with the huge option strangle must have made! Needless to say, I was not only relieved by my gains, but I was hooked on options!

PAY (Buy CALL to Open)

I immediately jumped back into the mix by purchasing a JAN 10 CALL on PAY (Verifone Corp) with a strike price of $15 per share at a net cost of $159.70, which was really more than I wanted to risk on my second option, but I did so nonetheless. I was willing to write off the cost as a part of my education if the call expired worthless. The ticker symbol for the option was PAYAC. Like AIG, Verifone was a company that I had already made a nice little profit on, and I had some seller's remorse for getting out too early. But unlike AIG, Verifone was not sitting on the verge of bankruptcy, so I jumped in by purchasing a more costly JAN CALL to open when the contract was priced at $1.50.

I chose Verifone because I had been in and out of the stock profitably a couple of times, and was very familiar with the company and its products. I was wary of the market, though, and bailed out of the stock when the whole market began to head south again. While my last sale left me with a total 7.75% gain annualized at almost 10%, I felt that I had sold out far too early. Adding insult to injury, shortly after I sold it at $13.94 PAY was upgraded by a few Wall Street analysts, and while I didn't want to buy it back for more than I had sold it, I didn't want to completely lose out on the impending potential upside. So I considered an option to increase my gain and possibly buy the stock back in the future at lower than market price. I did my research and finally made my decision to buy a single JAN 10 CALL on PAY with a strike price of $15 for $1.50 per contract. Since the contract represented 100 shares my total cost was $1.50 x 100 = $150 + $9.70 commission = $159.70. That is what it cost me to buy a contract that would allow me to purchase PAY shares at $15 at a time when I believed the stock could go to $18 or even $20 per share. At the time I purchased the contract, shares of PAY were trading at about $14.15. My hope was that the underlying stock would rise all the way to $20 or more and I could exercise the option and make a quick $327.30 for a ROI of 205% - and that wouldn't be bad for a short term $159.70 "test" investment!

At the time I had become quite obsessed with the prospect of making lots of money with options, and when PAY reached $15.67 per share I did some calculations to see how much I could make by exercising my option now that it was safely "in the money" with the shares selling above the strike price. I discovered that if I exercised the option at that point, I would *lose* $105, because it cost me over $150 to buy the option! I had not yet calculated my break even point! This concerned me, because I had recently learned that fully 90% of all CALL options will ultimately expire worthless. But upon further scrutiny of my option I learned that bidders had pushed up the price of my option. I discovered that even though – *at that point in time* – had I exercised the option I would have lost money, I could still make an immediate profit on my option by *selling the call to close the position.* So I immediately sold the option for $2.25 per contract for a total of $215.30, and after commissions paid for both getting in and out of the position I ended up with a gain of $55.60 or 34%. That is a very real 34% gain on an investment that I held for only 19 days!

While it is true that most calls will expire worthless, *none* of my first three transactions did! In all three cases I was able to *sell the option to close my position*, and in two of those cases I made very significant gains on a percentage basis. My confidence was growing! Looking back at my models, here is a summary of how these initial call options played out:

STK	SYMBOL	OPTION	STRIKE	PRICE-O	COMM	OPEN	TYPE
AIG	UZLKU.o	CALL NOV (	2	-0.18	-9.70	-27.70	CBO
AIG	UZLAZ.o	CALL JAN 1	2.5	-0.01	-16.45	-26.45	CBO
PAY	PAYAC.0	CALL JAN 1	15	-1.50	-9.70	-159.70	CBO

PRICE-C	PRICE +/-	CLOSE	$GAIN	%ROI	P-SHR	%+-STK
0.25	38.89	15.30	-12.40	-44.77	-2.48	-124.00
0.16	1500.00	143.55	117.10	442.72	2.34	93.68
2.25	50.00	215.30	55.60	34.82	0.56	3.71

The four lines at top show the details of how I opened my positions for AIG and PAY. The column under "OPEN" is the price I paid for these options (negative to show cash outlay). The next four lines show how much of each premium was regained or lost when I sold these options to close my positions. The column under CLOSE shows the selling price, followed by my profit/loss in dollars and return on investment. And they said it couldn't be done with CALL options!

In all three of the above examples my maximum risk was limited to the amount I paid in premiums to purchase the options. That is the advantage of taking a *long* position in options (i.e., purchasing calls or puts to open). You can always *sell* the option later, and even if you don't your maximum loss will always be limited to the price of the option, while your maximum gain is theoretically unlimited. XYZ Corporation could rise to $1,000,000 per share while you are holding a call option to buy it for $1 per share. When you take a long position you always have the option to take some action, but you have no obligation whatsoever to do so. The downside of long call options, though, is that it is much harder to make money with them than it looks on the surface. The harsh reality is that most calls purchased to open will expire worthless, and if you just go out and buy a lot of calls with the simple hope that the underlying stock will rise in value, you will probably lose a lot of money. We all know that stock prices don't go up forever; there can and will be very wild swings in stock prices over time. I was very fortunate indeed in the case of my AIG calls that all of the elements necessary for a speculator driven increase in the price of the underlying stock fell into place at exactly the right time. I can assure you that while I made a very small profit on these options there were many, many other traders who lost many thousands, or even millions trading on these options at the time of the split.

I need to stress here that you should not confuse this kind of sale with that of selling a call to open a position, *which makes you the writer of the contract* – and obligated to buy or sell shares of the stock to the option holder at the strike price! But don't let the word *obligation* scare you away from writing contracts. Why fear an obligation to sell your stock if you were able to lock in a 50% gain annualized at 200%? Of course you would welcome this kind of obligation, and you can realize this potential by writing puts and calls! In the section that follows, I will show you exactly how to add an extra income stream to your brokerage account by writing *safe, sane, and simple* option contracts!

Section 7 – Selling Puts and Calls to Open

Let's start this section with an example of my very first attempt at what is generally considered the most conservative of all ways to trade in options while investing in stocks. This is called *writing a covered call.*

VLO (Valero – Sell Covered Call to Open)

When you *sell a call to open* you are assuming a *short* position. You are selling the right for the option holder to buy shares from you at the strike price anytime before expiration, and you are obligated to deliver those shares when the holder exercises the option. If it is exercised at a strike price of $10 when the market price is $100 you would have a huge paper loss, but you might still have a gain if you had bought your shares for $5 and held them while selling the call. This contract is a called a *covered call.* A properly written covered call will always pay you a handsome, immediate premium that you can keep, and will only be exercised at a pre-determined strike price that gives you another handsome gain; you can't lose! If on the other hand you sell a naked call, *your potential loses are real and unlimited*! So my general rule of thumb is this: if you are going to sell a call to open, make sure it is a covered call!

Here is a simple example of my first sale of a covered call. The underlying stock was Valero (VLO) the big refinery that I bought into at $23.05 per share in January of 2009. I thought it was a good purchase at the time because gasoline prices always go up, but what I failed to realize is that when the price of crude oil rises, profit margins for oil refineries like Valero are squeezed. In the tumultuous 9 months that followed, VLO moved down to trade in the range of $16-$18 per share. I was in the red, and the price of the stock was going sideways.

This recipe is the perfect scenario for selling a covered call. So I sold a single JAN 10 CALL contract with a strike price of $25 at a time when the stock was selling at about $18. At the time, my stock position was $980 in the red, but by selling the January call I pocketed a quick $69.50, and I would only have to sell my shares if they rose above $25. I seriously doubted that would happen by January, but if it did I would gain $550, a nice 12% profit annualized at almost 30% while keeping the $69.50 premium. This might seem like very small potatoes in terms of a net profit, but these potatoes were free – money that I pocketed that actually *reduced* my risk while increasing my profit potential!

STK	SYMBOL	OPTION	STRIKE	PRICE-O	COMM	OPEN
VLO	VLBAY.x	CALL JAN 10	25	0.40	-10.45	69.55

EXEC $	TODAY $	$GAIN	%ROI	P-SHR	%+-STK
5000	5000	56.55	81.31	0.28	1.13

ICO (International Coal – Sell PUTS to Open)

Once I realized how safe-and-sane selling covered calls could be, I didn't hesitate to jump into selling covered puts as well. When I say "covered put" I mean selling *a contract that obligates you to purchase stock* in the future should the holder choose to exercise the contract. Your position is "covered" by cash or other securities placed on "hold" in your brokerage account specifically for the purpose of purchasing these shares if the option is exercised; otherwise you would be "naked."

I saw some income potential in my coal stocks. I really think that coal stocks will take off big sometime next year. For the last few months they have been moving slowly, but they were moving to the upside. I own two different coal stocks; one is an American mining company, while the other is a Chinese company. I didn't want to overextend myself, but I figured I could safely sell some *in the money puts* on the American company (ICO - International Coal Group) in order to generate some immediate income, and hold off on selling against the Chinese coal stock (YZC – YanZhou Coal). So in October, when ICO was selling for $4.50 I sold 7 MAR 10 PUTs with a strike of $5 to earn a premium of $720.00. This is money that went straight into my pocket, lowering my overall cost of purchasing ICO stocks!

With the added cushion of this premium, I would make a profit even if the stock dropped to $3.98 before the option was exercised. But since I believed the stock was headed north and would soon be red hot, I wasn't concerned with this.

I was so comfortable with my decision, in fact, that I took it one step further – literally – by selling *even more* puts on ICO. This time I sold 4 JUN 10 PUTs with the same strike price of $5. My thinking was that if ICO was over $5 in March, it would certainly be more than $5 per share in June! If not, I would have plenty of time to take corrective measures. So I sold the JUN 10 PUT contracts for ICO at a price of $1.00 per contract and pocketed an additional $388.05 in premiums. Here is a summary of those puts sold to open my position:

STK	SYMBOL	OPTION	STRIKE	PRICE-O	COMM	OPEN	TYPE
ICO	ICOOA	PUT MAR 1ı	5	1.05	-14.20	720.80	**PSO**
ICO	ICORA.o	PUT JUN 1C	5	1.00	-11.95	388.05	**PSO**

The beauty of this deal is that I get to put the premiums earned into my interest earning or capital appreciation account immediately. The maximum gain is the sum of the premiums earned plus whatever additional appreciation is realized in the price of the underlying stock. There is only limited protection against a sudden collapse in stock price, though, and my maximum loss would be the sum of shares put to me times the strike price minus the premiums received. Since my puts are for 1100 shares my maximum loss would be $5500 minus $1098.95 in premiums, for a total of $4401.05. That seems like a big risk to take in exchange for an $1108.85 premium, but if I bought the stock outright my maximum loss would be $5500 plus commissions paid! My general rule of thumb is to never sell puts on stocks that I wouldn't want to own!

MEA (Metalico – Sell PUT to Open)

Remember how I profited by selling a call to open a short position against my 200 shares of Valero (VLO) when the contract sold for .40 and I earned $69 in premiums, locking in a 12% gain annualized at almost 30%. In exchange, I granted the contract holder the right to buy VLO away from me at $25 per share, but I doubted this would happen, because I could not see the stock rising much above $20 in the remaining time of the contract. This was an excellent deal for me. Even though the premium I earned was relatively small, the deal was solidly in my favor and added nicely to my overall gains.

Now let's consider Metalico (MEA) a metal recycling company stock that I had eagerly purchased prior to the global economic crisis. Metal recycling was not the best business to be in during the meltdown; most companies in this sector took a severe beating with many falling quickly and irrevocably into bankruptcy. I bought MEA at $15.50 per share, and watched in agony as the shares dropped all the way down to $3.95. I still believed, however, that of all the metal recycling firms out there, Metalico had a good chance for complete recovery, so I bought more of it on the way down, and with 500 shares I was able to lower my average purchase price to $6.30 per share.

The problem was, even after the strongest stock rally of the last 50 years - between March of 2009 and September of 2009 - when the Dow Jones Industrial Average rose from around 7500 to 9500, MEA remained flat and I was still seriously in the red. So I decided to sell some put options to offset some of this loss. I am not sure this was the best thing to do, given the advice that I have already given you, and that is to never sell a put on a stock unless you really, really want to own that stock. But I found a put on MEA that was irresistible.

SYMBOL	OPTION	STRIKE	PRICE-O	COMM	OPEN	TYPE
MEAPA.o	PUT APR 10	5	1.37	-12.70	670.48	**PSO**

I sold five MEA APR 10 PUT contracts with a strike price of $5 and pocketed a $670.48 premium. While this sale put me at risk of having to purchase 500 more shares, the premium reduced the effective price that I would pay for those shares to $3.66 per share, and averaging this against the shares I already owned reduced my average share price to $5.65.

My thinking at the time that I sold this contract was that there should be little chance of the holder exercising the put against me unless the price of the shares dropped below $3.66 (my break even point). What I failed to consider, though, was that there might be other holders of this same contract who purchased it at a different point in time, and at a much lower price than the ones that I sold. This is important because when options are exercised it is not in such as way as the holder of a contract will put shares back to the very same person who sold the contract. Instead, the Options Clearing Corporation assigns exercised options in a more random way, and when the holder of a put exercises the option the actual assignment can be made to anybody who had sold the put to open a contract with the same strike price and expiration date. The amount of premium I received is immaterial. The option could be exercised against me by anyone who held the contract, even if it cost them next to nothing to purchase it. So with MEA trading today at $4.00 per share, there is a very good chance that the option will be exercised against me unless the share price rises above the $5 strike price before April, 2010.

Today (November 10, 2009) Metalico announced some "significant improvements" in their results for the 3rd quarter of 2009. Still, the value of their stock sank another .05, or 1% in response to the news. Being a little concerned about the future prospects of this stock, I decided to place an order to sell five APR 10 CALL options with a strike price of $5 at .55 per contract, for a net gain of $262.40. Since I had already sold a put on this stock, the additional sale of a call established a *call-put combination*. Now, if I add this premium to the previous $670.48 that I pocketed from the puts that I sold earlier, then my average cost for any new shares that I might have to purchase if the puts are exercised will be reduced to about $3.16 per share. Of course, should MEA rise above $5 then I could see my shares called away from me, but because of the premiums earned I will still have realized a 9% gain. If any case, I would keep the $932.80 premium, reducing my overall risk and profit potential. But that order expired unfilled.

VALE (Sell PUT and CALL to Open)

By now I am sure you are beginning the think the same thing that I thought shortly after my initial successes earning an income from the sale of puts or calls against an underlying stock. What occurred to me was this: If I can make money selling just puts against stocks, could I make money selling *put-call combinations* all the time? After giving this question considerable thought I came to the conclusion that I could in fact safely sell them so long I fully understood the implications of writing these contract combinations.

When you sell a PUT contract you are selling someone the right to sell you shares of a stock at some future price, and you are obligated to purchase them if they exercise that right. If the share price rises above the strike price the holder will not exercise the option, and you will simply keep your premiums. But if the price drops beneath the strike price, he might decide to exercise the option and you must purchase the shares.

When you sell a covered call you are selling the right for the holder to buy shares from you at the strike price on or before the expiration date. If you write your contract correctly, you simply cannot lose money on a covered call, but your gain is limited to the premiums earned plus whatever additional gain you earned as your stock rose to meet the option strike price.

When you write a put your losses are limited to the number of shares covered by the contracts times the strike price minus the total premiums gained, and this could be substantial! *Never* sell puts on a stock that is so shaky that the company might go bankrupt tomorrow! If you were to sell a put to open on XYZ Corporation for $10 a share and its price drops to 0, you would loose $10.00 x 100 = $1000 times the number of contracts, minus the premium you pocketed. If you sold just one contract you would stand to loose $1,000.00, but if you sold 1,000 contracts your loss would exceed a million dollars!

Then again, if a put is exercised against you and you are forced buy a stock at $10 per share while it is trading at $5 on the open market, you do not have a real loss. First, by virtue of the premium earned, you actually paid less than $5.00 per share. Secondly, even if you do have a paper loss, that "loss" is really only a higher cost basis per share than the current market supports. As long as the company is healthy, the value of its shares will ultimately rise, and you may still realize a profit. You can sell put-call combinations on a stock if it is an investment grade product and your strike prices are sufficiently out of the money, but you should only do so if the premiums are justified when calculated against prevailing interest rates.

To illustrate, I had bought what seemed like a rational stock on the advice of a TV business program announcer who made a good argument for buying the stock when it was selling at $41.50 per share. I picked up fifty shares of VALE – the giant Brazilian mining company - at that price and watched in disbelief as the market for steel collapsed and the price of the stock dropped to $17.75. Figuring it couldn't go any lower I snatched up another 50 shares and watched as the stock moved sideways between $17 and $22 per share over the next six months, going nowhere fast. I concluded that it couldn't go any lower, so I then elected to purchase another 100 shares at $21 figuring it would neutralize the high cost basis established by my initial purchase price of $41.50. This set my average price per share at $25.31. Over the next year and a half the stock rose only a little and then travelled sideways between $23 and $26 for the two years after the big stock meltdown of 2007-08. I knew this stock would rise with time, and I considered how I might use options to reduce my exposure in the interim and possibly improve my profit potential in the future.

It was then that I realized that I could sell both put and calls on VALE in order to double recoup some of my losses! This simple strategy was to sell an out of the money put on VALE while simultaneously selling an out of the money call. By doing this I pocketed $300.00 in premiums, reducing my exposure a little bit, but every lit bit would help!

The put I sold gave the holder the right to sell me 200 shares of VALE at $22.00 per share – a price I thought of as just beneath downside resistance, and a fair price to pay. Since Brazil's economy was strong I seriously doubted that VALE stock would ever drop below this price as the global economic recovery began. I felt very safe with this decision.

The call I sold gave the holder the right to buy shares from me at $27.50 per share, and that gave me a nice 15% gain on my original investment, not including the premiums that I pocketed. The magic of this strategy was that it lowered the price of any shares I might have to purchase to significantly *less* than the strike price of $22.00; my actual purchase price would be $21.73. If, on the other hand, I had to sell my shares, the price I would receive would be well above the $27.50 strike price – I would really be receiving $28.03 for almost a $20% gain. And whether or not an option was exercised, I would keep the nearly $300 in premiums I collected, at a 100% gain!

What bothered me a few weeks later, though, was that VALE was now on a roll – and I thought there might be much more of upside to be realized than I originally bargained for when I sold the $27.50 call. So when the time seemed right I exercised another options strategy that gave me much greater upside potential while pocketing yet another premium! The way I did this was to "roll up" my call option to a higher strike price. To do this I first bought back my JAN 10 $27.5 CALL to close my position for $508.45 - a $388.90 cents *loss* over the premium I gained when I first sold it for $119.55. But then I *sold* a new JAN 11 CALL with a strike price of $35 for a total of $557.70, thus regaining all of my loss and then some! The $50 earned here coupled with the $167.55 I pocketed on the DEC 10 put gave me a higher premium of $336! Better yet, the shares that I held now could potentially appreciate another $7.50 per share before they could be called away from me!

This would give me a whopping 44% profit on the stock. By selling a put-call combination, and then rolling up my call, I was able to increase both my immediate profits as well as my potential future profits without increasing my risk!

Below is a summary of my VALE option positions. I am hoping these three open positions will all simply expire:

STK	SYMBOL	OPTION	STRIKE	PRICE-O	COMM	OPEN	TYPE
VALE	RIOXX.o	PUT DEC 10	22.5	0.89	-10.45	167.55	**PSO**
VALE	RFPAY.o	CALL JAN 10	27.5	0.65	-10.45	119.55	**CSO**
VALE	VOHAG	CALL JUN 11	35	2.84	-10.45	557.55	**CSO**

Before selling the VOHAG call to open on VALE with that really nice big premium, I closed out my previous RFPAY position as shown below:

PRICE-C	PRICE +/-	CLOSE	GAIN	ROI%
-2.49	283.08	-508.45	-388.90	-325.30

Can you see the beauty of these strategic maneuvers? At the time I sold the options I had only about a $300 gain in VALE. The stock had travelled sideways for so long in barely positive territory but I still believed it had a great deal of upside potential. The market was so unsettled, though, that I decided to sell the call option to possibly sell the stock at an adjusted price of $28.03 and be satisfied with a nice gain, even if it were less than stellar. And if the market did drop instead and the put was exercised against me, I would be happy to buy more of this stock at a discount from $22.50 – the real price would be only $21.73 a share. This would further reduce my average costs while I pocketed the nice premium I received on the call. But then I realized that I really wanted to hold onto VALE, and by "rolling up" the call option to a later expiration date and higher strike price I was able to earn an even higher premium while increasing my maximum gain from an average return of 20% to a fantastic potential return of 44%.

It is important to realize that the real goal of a strategy such as this is to maximize income from premiums, hoping that the options will not be exercised and that your shares will continue to appreciate. The downside of this strategy is that it limits your profit to the premiums earned plus gains on your already profitable stock, but it offers no protection against a sudden, deep drop in stock prices. If you picked a shaky stock, you could be forced to buy shares that drop to $0 in value.

C (Citicorp – Sell PUT and CALL to open)

I used a similar strategy against my Citicorp stock. Like everyone else I jumped into "C" at the beginning of a long and pain downward slide. Shown below is a table listing my stock transactions for "C" prior to taking an options position. My entry point was 100 shares at $23.60 per share, and one year later the shares were selling between $2.50 and $3.50 per share. I bought 900 more at these prices to reduce my average cost. Here is the history of those purchases:

TRAN DATE	SHR_BUY	SHR_SEL	SHARE-$	INVESTED	SOLD	DAYS
2008/04/09	100	0	23.60	2360.00	0	569
2009/03/19	200	0	3.88	776.00	0	225
2009/03/19	500	0	2.60	1300.00	0	225
2009/06/18	200	0	3.12	624.00	0	134

Investing in 100 shares at $23.60 back in April of 2008, and then watching as the market meltdown whittled this value down to $2.50 a year later was a very painful experience, both financially and emotionally. When the market finally made a little bounce back after the first news indicators that we might be at the bottom of the recession I resolved to stick with my decision to hold the stock until I could eventually turn a profit.

For a while I was above water with C, but then the stock began a lengthy sideways journey that had me sometimes in the black and sometimes in the red, with no clear indication of where the stock might be going, although it seemed to prefer the range of $4.40 - $4.80 per share. At $4.65 per share my position was $381 dollars in the red. So, after realizing I could sell a *put-call combination* to close this deficit I sold these next two options to generate some immediate income and elevate my position just a little further into the black.

STK	SYMBOL	OPTION	STRIKE	PRICE-O	COMM	OPEN	TYPE
C	CCH.o	CALL MAR 10	8	0.15	-16.45	133.55	**CSO**
C	CMW.X	PUT JAN 10	4	0.27	-16.45	253.55	**PSO**

The immediate tangible effect of selling these contracts was to place $387 directly into my brokerage account and this lowered my breakeven point on C from $5.03 per share down to $4.65 per share. I was immediately back in the black!

My thinking when I sold the March call was that if the stock went to $8.00 per share in March I would be happy to sell it for $8048 given that I only paid $4672 for the shares; that is a 72% gain! I also reasoned that the stock price would actually have to rise above $8.12 for the buyer to recoup the premium that he paid to purchase the option. Of course, I now know that the reality is this: if the stock price closes above $8 it *probably* will be called away from me because there are other holders of the contract out there who probably paid a lot less than the $133.55 premium I pocketed when I sold the call. But in the meantime, the premium was mine, working in my favor!

Conversely, my thinking when I sold the JAN 10 PUT was that if the stock dropped down to $4 and it was put to me at that amount, I would be quite happy because first, I believe the stock will soon go back up past $5 per share, and second, the real cost for any shares put to me would be only $3.60 per share – a nice discount. Again, my thinking was that the buyer of this contract will probably not put the shares to me unless the price drops below $3.60 per share. If he puts to me when shares are selling above $3.60, then he will not recover the full amount of the premium he paid to purchase the put option. But I now know that it is very possible that the shares will be put to me if the stock price drops just slightly below $4.

To summarize all this, if the stock price *stays below* the call's $8 strike price then the call will expire worthless to the buyer and I will keep my shares. If it hits the strike price I will make a 72% gain on the sale of those shares. If the stock price *stays above* the put's $4 strike price then that option will expire worthless. If it falls below the strike price I will have to buy the shares covered by the contract, but I will pay a price that I established myself as the fair value of the shares, and that will be at a significant discount because of the nice premium I collected when I sold the put option. In every case, I will keep the premiums I earned when I sold the contracts.

So either way, I expect that I will make money on these options. Here is how the GAIN and ROI of the options on Citicorp will look if they are exercised at strike price:

EXEC $	TODAY $	$GAIN	%ROI	P-SHR	%+-STK
8000	8000	120.55	90.27	0.12	1.51
4000	4000	240.55	94.87	0.24	6.01

The gain is not a reflection of the gain or loss I realized as a result of *stock trades*; rather, this column reflects how much of my *original premium earned* when I opened the position was retained at the end of the day. You will recall that my actual gains on the sale of my C shares if the call were exercised against me at a strike price of $8 per share would be $3,300 plus the $387 premium earned when I sold the contracts, which is a whopping 72% percent gain! The P-SHR column shows how much this premium retention added to the value of each share covered by the contract.

General Electric (GE PUT Sell to Open)

Well, why should I stop now? I was having so much success with selling puts and calls that I decided to extend myself and sell some puts against another equity I no longer owned. I had profited nicely on previous trades of GE earning about 20% in just three months, but now I was completely out of that stock. I wanted back in, but not at a price higher than my last exit price which was about $14.50 a share. Rather than risking my profits, I decided to sell five JAN 10 PUT contracts with a strike price of $12.50 for .31 per contract, and this netted me a really nice $142.30 premium at a time when GE was trading at over $16.50 per share, $4 over my strike price! I thought it inconceivable that, riding on the back of a strong stock rally, the stock would drop back to the strike price, but I actually hoped that it would! So it was a no-brainer for me sell the put with a strike of $12.50. It was a premium paid to me as pure profit, really, because I would have purchased the stock anyway had it dropped back down to $12.50 per share. But now, with the cushion of the $1.42 per share premium stored safely in my pocket, if the put were exercised against me at the strike price of $12.50 I would really pay only $11.08 per share, well below my last exit price!

SILVER ETF (SLV PUT Sell to Open)

At about this same time I also learned that my Schwab brokerage account did not limit my option trades to individual stocks. I had other options, so to speak, and I discovered that I could also use options strategies against Exchange Traded Funds - mutual funds that trade in real time just as stocks do.

One such ETF that I had made a lot of money on was SLV - the ETF that is backed by silver holdings. In less than a year I had parlayed my investment in SLV into a 27% gain, and - living by my 25% per year profit rule - I placed a stop-limit order to sell my shares in this ETF and lock in my gain at

25%. The stock took a dip and my order was executed, but shortly thereafter SLV started another steady bullish rise as the value of the dollar continued to slide. Now, with both gold and silver prices soaring, I once gain suffered seller's remorse. I wanted back in, but not at the risk of giving up my profits!

So what I decided to do instead was to sell two put contracts on SLV, one being an APR 2010 PUT with a strike of $15 at .90 cents per contract for a premium of $142.30, while the second was a JAN 2011 PUT with a strike of $15 at $1.60 per contract for a premium of $399.55. So in essence I earned almost $550.00 to do nothing more than collect the money, then wait and hope for the price of SLV to drop to the strike price - a price that I would happily pay in order to get back into the game. If the price of SLV continue to rise I will continue to sell far out of the money puts against it until that time, I imagine, when my premiums earned might actually exceed the price of any shares I purchase. It is possible with this strategy of selling puts, to eventually purchase stocks for nothing!

China Direct Corp (CDII – Sell CALL to Open)

Just to be sure that everyone gets into the pool together, lets mention one more CALL that I sold to open. This was a simple, no-brainer in my eyes. I had purchased 200 shares of

China Direct Corporation (CDII) at $1.50, and it simply went nowhere. And it didn't look like it was going to go anywhere anytime soon. So I sold a CALL option against it that allowed me to pocket $39.55. Believe it or not, this tiny premium turned my position in the stock from a negative one to positive. It gave me an immediate profit while I waited for someone to buy the stock away from me at an even greater profit! And here is how that one traded to open:

SYMBOL	OPTION	STRIKE	PRICE-O	COMM	OPEN	TYPE
CDSCZ.X	CALL MAR 10	2.5	0.25	-10.45	39.55	**CSO**

Let me make one more very important point – one that I should have made at the beginning of this section. Every contract that I write is covered; i.e., they are backed either by stocks I own or cash in my account. When you write a covered call or put, you must *hold* that cash or equities in your account until the option is settled. You can think of those assets as being a "time deposit," and the premium is the interest earned for this deposit. For example, let's revisit my APR 10 MEA PUT. To satisfy that put I needed to maintain a $2500 balance in my account until the put was settled or expired, a total of 176 days. I earned a $670 premium, which is a 26.82% return on the $2500 held in my account. But since the duration of the hold was only 176 days my annualized rate of return on the option alone was actually an astonishing 55.62%!

Section 8 – Reducing Risk with Spreads

When I sold the put to open on AOB I was certain that I made a great decision. I picked up over $812 dollars by selling a put that gave the holder the right to sell (PUT) 500 shares to me at $5 per share - $2.50 per share less than the average I had paid for shares already owned. If the shares were put to me at $5 I would enjoy that discount and, the $812 premium earned would be extra icing on the cake! This effectively reduced the break even point on those shares to $3.40 per share. As long as the shares were trading at above $3.40 at the time they were PUT to me I would make money or break even. If they were trading at less than $3.40 per share at the time they were PUT to me, then technically I would be in the red but I would own the shares and possibly earn a profit on them in the future.

But then I thought the unthinkable; what would happen if by some catastrophic event, the price AOB shares dropped to $0? In the midst of the meltdown this was suddenly happening to much bigger Corporations in markets all over the world. With auto manufactures, giant banks, insurance and finance companies and the like vaporizing overnight I was suddenly deeply concerned. If AOB's stock suddenly collapsed (again) I would be obligated to buy 500 *more* shares at $5 per share, and they might be utterly worthless at that time! Since I had collected $812 in premiums when I sold the put, I could subtract that amount from the $2500 cost of fulfilling my obligation, but this would still result in a *real* $1688 loss!

In thinking about this I suddenly realized that I was engaged in some pretty risky trading. Of course, I knew there were risks all along, but I hadn't given it much thought. I was assuming a very aggressive position in which I sold short both puts and calls on the same stock with my goal being to retain relatively small premiums due to 0% volatility in stock price. The danger was this: I was subjecting myself to substantial, even unlimited losses if the stock moved markedly in either direction! As long as the stock stayed between the strike prices I did well, but the further the stock price moved outside of this range, either to the upside or the downside, the more money I would actually lose! Ouch! Is there anything I might possibly do to mitigate this potential loss and protect my position?

Well one thing I could always do is buy my put options back to close my position. I might find though, that the price of my put option has risen rapidly as the price of the underlying shares dropped. While I sold it for $812, I might find that it will cost me much more than that to buy it back. Still, if the stock is in a freefall then taking an $800 loss by purchasing an identical option to close my position at twice its original price is much better than taking the $1688 loss if the shares fell all the way to zero. But in order to succeed at this I would quite literally have to be follow my stock prices and option positions on a minute by minute basis as the expiration date drew closer.

Fortunately there are other, more conservative and safer strategies that protect against big losses in ways that selling short puts and calls alone cannot. Most traders who are not 100% certain of their conviction will attempt to mitigate their potential losses should they be wrong by hedging their investment when they open their position in the first place. They will do this with what is called a *spread*, and this involves buying an option to open a long position on a stock, and then selling an option on the same stock to open a short position in the opposite direction at the same time. Creating a spread in this way will have the double effect of limiting your losses, but also limiting your potential gains. Without getting too technical, let me illustrate how this might work.

Recall for a moment that I sold 5 JAN 2010 PUT contracts giving the holder the right to sell me 500 shares of AOB Corp at $5.00 per share on or before the third Friday in January 2011. At the time I sold the contracts the underlying stock was trading at $4.50, meaning the contract was "in the money" since the market price was already lower than the strike price. Since the expiration date was still almost sixteen months away, there was both *intrinsic value and time value* reflected in the price of the option, which I sold for $1.65 x 500 shares - $12.70 commission for a net profit of $812.30, a nice premium indeed.

When I sold this put my main goal was to capture the premium. My expectation was that by January 2011 AOB stock, a Chinese pharmaceutical stock, would be selling well above $5 per share, and that the option would simply expire worthless. But what if the stock goes down? If it does then it will cost me more to buy the contract back than I earned by selling it, and if I don't buy it back then my exposure to the declining stock will increase. This is a risky position to assume!

Now, suppose when I sold the put I also *bought* a JAN 11 PUT option on the same stock, but at a lower strike price of $3.50. Since the strike price is lower than the current market value of the underlying shares the option is "out of the money," and its price will be significantly less than the "in the money" put I sold earlier. In this case, the price of a JAN 11 PUT is only $.50, so to buy 5 contracts would cost $.50 x 500 + $12.70 commission for a total of $262.70.

This contract gives me the right - *but not the obligation* - to sell 500 shares of AOB to the writer of the contract for $3.50 per share. Now, if you subtract the $262.70 that I *paid* for the put I purchased from the $812.30 premium I *earned* from the put I sold, then I will have a *net credit* of $550.30 - still a sizable premium to pocket. What I basically did was establish a "credit spread" in which I gave up $262.70 of my $812.30 earned premium in order to buy "insurance" on my position through the purchase of the put option. This particular kind of spread is called a *credit spread* since the position resulted in me earning and retaining a premium.

Now, if the price of the AOB is below $5.00 per share just before the expiration date I may have to buy 500 shares at $5 for an outlay of $2500. Since I kept a $550 premium, though, my actual cost will be $1950 - about $3.90 per share - still above my breakeven point. As long as the stock is trading above $3.90 I will make a profit.

If the stock stabilizes and rises, I could sell the put I bought to close that position and regain some of the premium I paid for that option, thus increasing my gains. But if the stock were to fall below $3.50 per share, I could sell the 500 shares that were PUT to me at $5 for $3.50 per share. This would leave me with a loss of $750. But since the spread I established left me with a net credit of $550, my loss would actually be reduced to $200, and this is the *maximum* that I could loose. While this does work in practice, the reality is that in the case of AOB I was after the *maximum premium*. If I had wanted to leverage to capitalize on stock appreciation, then I would have purchased an at-the-money call; I would not have sold an in-the-money put! But my primary goal was to capture the premium. I fully believed the stock would rise - not fall - so I didn't bother buying insurance.

If your goal were to capitalize on stock appreciation while minimizing risk, a bull spread would be the means to achieve this, and could be established as follows. You would first *buy* an at-the-money JAN 10 CALL, for example, to purchase shares of XYZ at a strike price of $50 for a total contract price of say, $100. You would then *sell* a JAN 10 CALL that gives the buyer the right to purchase shares from you at $60 per share, and this might net you $35 per contract. The total cost of your position would then be $100-$35=$65.00. This is called a *bull debit spread,* since you bought a *long* position on the stock and *paid* a premium for that call. By selling the out-of-the-money call you reclaimed *some* of that premium, and you also reduced your potential loss to the *net cost of your position* should the price of the underlying stock suddenly collapse. But this position also limits your potential profit, and if the stock soars the maximum profit you could expect to earn will be the difference between the two strike prices minus the net cost of the position. In this case that would be ($60-$50=$10) x 100 shares = $1000 - $35 contract price = $765.00 and this is your maximum possible gain.

If you are bearish on a stock you can also assume a bear spread position in the same way. First buy an at-the-money put on the stock, then sell an out-of-the-money put with the same expiration date. Once again, your maximum loss would be the net cost of the premiums to assume the position, and your maximum gain would be the difference in strike prices times the number of shares minus the net cost of the contract.

It is also possible to establish a *credit spread,* in which case you are left with a positive net premium, and this would be your *maximum gain.* Excluding commissions, the maximum loss on a credit spread is calculated as the difference of the two strike prices minus any premiums earned. But an in-depth, discussion of the these spreads and other hedging strategies such as time spreads, horizontal and diagonal spreads, straddles and strangles elevates the discussion to one reserved for expert option traders, and goes way beyond the scope of this book, which discusses simple strategies for the novice trader.

In addition, a detailed analysis of buying protection in almost every case shows that, while it is a very sound practice when selling puts on highly volatile, "C" or "B" class stocks, there is very little value in buying protection if the underlying security is investment-grade. If you as an investor have very strong convictions about the direction a stock will move, you will surrender enormous earning potential when you buy "insurance" in the form of sophisticated spreads. Still, there are times when opening a spread is absolutely your best move, so shown below are examples of four basic types of spreads.

CNTS STK	OPTION	EXPIRE	STRIKE	PRICE-O	COMM	OPEN	TYPE
Vertical Spread							
10 PAY	CALL	Jan-11	36	1.10	-16.45	1083.55	**CSO**
10 PAY	CALL	Jan-11	37	-0.75	-16.45	-766.45	**CBO**
20				0.35	-32.90	317.10	
Diagonal Spread							
2 SLV	CALL	Jan-11	23	-1.81	-10.45	-372.45	**CBO**
2 SLV	PUT	Apr-11	18	0.45	-10.45	79.55	**PSO**
4				-1.36	-20.90	-292.90	
Strangle							
1 AIG	CALL	Jan-12	65	-2.60	-9.70	-269.70	**CBO**
1 AIG	PUT	Jan-12	60	-2.50	-9.70	-259.70	**PBO**
2				-5.10	-19.40	-529.40	
Straddle							
2 CAAS	CALL	Jan-12	15	-2.75	-10.45	-560.45	**CBO**
2 CAAS	PUT	Jan-12	15	-2.25	-10.45	-460.45	**PBO**
4				-5.00	-20.90	-1020.90	

The vertical spread (having the same expiration date but different strike prices) is also called a "bear credit spread." You believe that the price of PAY is going to drop, so you sell 10 call contracts with a strike of 36 to pocket a very nice $1083.55 premium. To protect yourself against the possibility of the stock going UP in price you buy 10 call contracts with a higher strike price, and you pay $766.45, leaving you will a net credit of $317.10 after commissions.

Now see if you can determine what the strategy might be for the other three examples, all of which are "debit" spreads (so you know you are not going after the premiums).

I am a firm believer in the practice of using stop-limit orders to protect you against a loss of profits. Simply place an order with your broker to start selling your stocks if they drop below the specified *stop* price, but in no case sell them below the specified *limit* price. For example, suppose you have XYZ Corporation stock and it is currently selling at $50 per share. You originally purchased it at $25 per share. You wish to protect some of this 100% gain, so you place a stop-limit order with your broker to start selling shares if the price drops to the $47 *stop* price, but to sell no shares below the $45 limit price. This guarantees that your profit on any stocks sold will be at least 80% and you will have paid nothing for this protection.

Section 9 - Conclusions

When you trade in options you may pursue any of a number of strategies to increase your profits while minimizing your investment risks. Your goal might be to earn immediate additional income from stock that you already own without selling any of those shares. In this case you would sell *far out of the money calls* against the shares you already own. Your goal would be for the option to expire worthless to the buyer and you pocket the premium paid.

You might wish to buy shares of a particular stock at a discount from its current selling price. In this case you would *sell covered out of the money puts* on the stock that would allow you to pocket a premium while you wait for the stock to drop below the price you are willing to pay. You can do this safely without buying an additional put for protection so long as the underlying stock is investment grade. If it is less than investment grade, then you should seriously consider a setting up a spread when selling such puts.

You might want to unload some stock that has not been performing to your complete satisfaction. You would do this by first determining the price that you are willing to sell it for, and then selling a near or perhaps in the money call option that will allow the holder to purchase it away from you should it reach that price. If you are concerned that the stock might fall below your break even point or "point of no return" you might also think about buying a put option that will allow you to sell the stock to the buyer at your minimum selling price.

You might wish to simply earn money through the trade of options alone, without ever buying stocks. Most people do this by simply buying call options on volatile stocks that they believe will move significantly upward before the expiration date of the option, and then selling the option for a profit. This is risky, though, because most such options expire worthless or are sold to close at a loss.

Finally, you might intend to simply protect yourself against a sudden and sustained loss in the value of your stock, in which case you would purchase put options at a strike price the protects your investment. Doing so involves paying a premium as a form of "insurance" to protect the stock against a deep drop in price. This works best if you have just taken a long position with the purchase of a stock that you expect will make a dramatic price move due to some forthcoming news such as an earnings report, a legal judgment, etc, but you are uncertain of the direction the stock will go.

The initial option positions that I opened (and which form the body of the case studies examined in this book) were based on my limited knowledge of options that I had acquired at that time. Since then (only a couple of short months later) I have learned a great deal more. In addition to online research of options trading, I also purchased a number of books that I pored over to further my understanding of options trading. In short, my research of options trading has been non-stop since my interest began, and I have learned a lot since opening my initial positions (which gave me a net credit of over $4,40.00).

What I have learned is this: My covered call positions, in which I sold call options giving the buyers the right to purchase from me shares of stock that I already owned at some future price that guaranteed me a very nice, pre-calculated rate of return were all very good decisions. The only exception to this is the call I sold on EROC, which I ended up buying back for a net debit of $14.40. I bought this call back to close because the company was upgraded by a number of analysts who also raised their target price on the stock to $7.50. So I bought back my call because I believed the upside potential is real and far surpasses the $80 in premiums I earned when I sold the option while the stock was still heading sideways. All in all, I stand firmly by all of my decisions to sell covered call options.

In the case of my sold PUTS my feelings are more mixed. At the time I sold these options I was really thinking only about the immediate income. The thought that I could make a quick $800 by selling an ITM (in the money) put against AOB completely overshadowed any consideration I gave to the idea that the company might in fact be a poor investment. On paper it looks good, although there have been discussions in the media about "management improprieties." When you read things like this and the stock then goes south you can't help but wonder if your decision was a wise one. This is the risk of greed that I discussed earlier.

I also doubled up on my puts for International Coal Group (ICO), selling a JAN 10 PUT with a strike of $5 as well as a MAR 10 PUT with a strike of $5. Both of these puts were in the money, with the stock trading at just under $5 when I sold the contracts. Greed blinded me to the fact, however, that the market had enjoyed an unprecedented, unparalleled rise since March - a full 9 months of gains - and this couldn't go on forever. This was a very bullish position for me to take, and while I am still very bullish on ICO, only time will tell if it will continue to rise past 5 as the market teeters on fears of a correction. Of course, I can close these positions if the stock drops below my break even for the position of $4.00 per share.

In a nutshell, the only option trades that I am little nervous about are the puts that I sold that might force me to buy additional shares of a stock that I really did not want to buy based on the fundamental intrinsic value of the company, but instead sold only to earn a premium that would reduce my average price paid per share with the hope of making an early exist when the stock moved into the black.

So the rule to follow when considering the sale of puts or calls is this: when it comes to selling puts, sell them only against blue chip stocks that you really, really want to own, and sell calls only against those stocks that you would not mind at all selling, given the profit that you calculated you will realize with their sale.

My philosophy for selling out of the money covered calls and covered puts is simple. It is the same "buy low sell high" strategy that I have used very successfully with volatile issues like commodities (AGU, SLV, and GLD) and big blue stocks that pay dividends but tend to trade sideways over time. By using puts and calls to purchase them I set my desired target price in advance and can pocket a nice premium while I wait for the stock to hit that target. It is similar to limit and stop-limit prices on orders, except you get paid handsomely to sit back and wait for the order to be exercised.

One other thing that you should be well aware of when trading options in either a margin or non-marginable account is this: the more puts you sell, the less cash you will have on hand for immediate stock purchases should an opportunity arise. For example, suppose you sell a standard put contract on XYZ Corporation with a strike price of $50 per share, and this option pays you a nice premium of $1,000. Even though your account will be immediately credited with this $1,000, $5,000 will be "frozen" in your account, *placed on hold* to pay for those 100 shares of XYZ should the holder of the contract elect to put them to you. So when you start selling a ton of puts, you are also reducing your liquid cash available for immediate stock purchases. Of course, you can always free up cash immediately by buying back the puts you sold to close these positions, but you might lose some of your premiums by doing this.

In short, you must always be mindful of how much money you are tying up in when you selling puts, and be sure that you actually comfortable with the idea of spending that much on the stock that could be put to you. In the case of calls, you must always be aware of the potential upside that you might be giving up if you write the call with a strike price to close to being "in the money."

To summarize, let's review all of my trades to date:

SYMBOL	TRAN DATE	INVESTED	SOLD	TYPE	NOTE
AIG.2	2009/07/15	26.45	0	CALL	CBO JAN 10 2.5 UZLAZ
AIG.2	2009/07/15	27.90	0	CALL	CBO JAN 10 2.5 UZLKU
AIG.2	2009/08/20	0.00	15.29	CALL	CSC JAN 10 2.5 UZLKU
AIG.2	2009/08/21	0.00	143.55	CALL	CSC JAN 10 2.5 UZLAZ
PAY.2	2009/09/04	159.70	0	CALL	CBO JAN 10 17 PAYAC
PAY.2	2009/09/23	0.00	215.3	CALL	CSC JAN 10 17 PAYAC
VALE.2	2009/09/28	0.00	119.55	CALL	CSO JAN 10 27.5 VALE RFPAYo.2
VLO.5	2009/09/28	0.00	69.55	CALL	CSO JAN 10 25 VLBAYo.5
C.2	2009/10/02	0.00	133.55	CALL	CSO MAR 10 8 CCH.o
GE.5	2009/10/06	0.00	142.30	PUT	PSO JAN 10 12.50 GEWMV
CDII.5	2009/10/07	0.00	39.55	CALL	CSO MAR 10 2.5 CDSCZ.X
MEA.2	2009/10/07	0.00	670.48	PUT	PSO APR 10 5 MEAPA.o
C.2	2009/10/08	0.00	253.55	PUT	PSO JAN 10 4 CMW
ICO.2	2009/10/08	0.00	720.80	PUT	PSO MAR 10 5 ICOOA
SLV.5	2009/10/08	0.00	169.55	PUT	PSO MAR 10 15 SLVPO
VALE.5	2009/10/09	0.00	167.55	PUT	PSO DEC 10 22.5 RIOXX (WRONG ACCOU
SLV.5	2009/10/13	0.00	309.55	PUT	PSO JAN 11 15 SLV XUXMO
AOB.2	2009/10/15	0.00	812.30	PUT	PSO JAN 11 5 AOB ZZDMA
EROC.5	2009/10/15	0.00	80.30	CALL	CSO APR 11 5 EROC EAUDA
EROC.5	2009/10/21	94.70	0.00	CALL	CBC APR 11 5 EROC EAUDA
ICO.5	2009/10/22	0.00	388.05	PUT	PSO JUN 10 5 ICO
VALE.2	2009/11/11	508.45	0.00	CALL	CBC JAN 10 27.5 VALE RFPAY
VALE.2	2009/11/11	0.00	557.55	CALL	CSO JAN 11 35 VALE VOHAG (ROLLUP FR
PAY.5	2009/11/23	0.00	548.05	PUT	PSO JAN 11 10 PAY XKXMB
VALE.5	2009/11/23	26.45	0.00	PUT	PBC DEC 09 22.5 VALE RIOXX closed to sel
C.2	2009/12/03	176.45	0	PUT	PBC JAN 10 4 C CMW.x
WATG.2	2009/12/10	239.70	0	CALL	CBO APR 10 12.5 WATG WQUDV
F.2	2009/12/17		830.27	PUT	PSO JAN 11 7.50 F OKFMU
GE.5	2009/12/22	17.70	0	PUT	PBC JAN 10 12.50 GEWMV to finance new I(
AGU.2	2010/01/05	0.00	300.29	PUT	PSO AGU JAN 11 45 VAVMI
SCHF.5	2010/01/05	0.00	669.54	PUT	PSO JAN 10 30 OSFMF (SCHWAB INTL EQ
VALE.2	2010/01/07	546.74	0	CALL	CBC JAN 11 35 VALE VOHAG (to sell JAN 1:
VALE.2	2010/01/07	0.00	749.55	CALL	CSO JAN 12 40 VALE YGJ
SLV.5	2010/01/08	56.45	0	PUT	PBC APR 10 15 SLVPO to sell WATG PUT
WATG.5	2010/01/08	0.00	668.05	PUT	PSO JUL 10 12.5 WATG WQUSV
YZC.5	2010/01/12	0.00	328.05	PUT	PSO JUL 10 17.5 YZC YZCSC
MEA.2	2010/01/14	0.00	123.8	PUT	PSO JUL 10 5 MEA MEASA
ICO.2	2010/01/20	854.20	0	PUT	PBC MAR 10 5 ICO ICOOA
ICO.2	2010/01/20	0.00	930.8	PUT	PSO SEP 10 5 ICO ICOUA ROLLUP
VLO.5	2010/01/26	0.00	139.55	CALL	CSO JAN 11 25 VLO VHBAE
ACH.5	2010/01/26	0.00	689.55	PUT	PCO JAN 12 20 ACH LCF
YZC.5	2010/01/27	611.95	0	PUT	PBC JUL 10 17.5 YZC YZCSC
YZC.5	2010/01/28	0.00	337.3	PUT	PSO JUL 10 15 YZC
T.4	2010/01/29	0.00	1457.05	PUT	PSO JAN 11 22.5 ATT VFEME (Elaines 18K)
XLU.4	2010/01/29	0.00	345.55	PUT	PSO JAN 11 28 XLU ORUMB
GE.5	2010/02/25	0.00	436.54	PUT	PSO SEP 10 14 GE GEW
AA.5	2010/02/25	0.00	277.29	PUT	PSO OCT 10 10 AA
WATG.5	2010/02/25	0.00	408.04	PUT	PSO OCT 10 7.5 WATG
SEED.2	2010/03/03	0.00	526.54	PUT	PSO AUG 10 7.5 SEED
VALE.2	2010/03/08	0.00	669.54	PUT	PUT JAN 12 25 VALE

BOUGHT   3346.84
SOLD   15443.67
DIFF   12096.83

DIFF = retained profit!

Now let's take a look at my actual results as of the last revision of this book. Here is a list of all of my open positions:

STK	SYMBOL	OPTION	EXPIRE	STRIKE	PRICE-O	COMM	OPEN	TYPE
	OPEN OPTIONS							
WATG	WQUDV	CALL	Apr-10	12.5	-2.30	-9.70	-239.70	**CBO**
VLO	VHBAE	CALL	Jan-11	25	0.75	-10.45	139.55	**CSO**
VALE	YGJ	CALL	Jan-12	40	3.80	-10.45	749.55	**CSO**
VALE	YGJ	PUT	Jan-12	25	3.40	-10.45	669.55	**PSO**
MEA	MEAPA.(	PUT	Apr-10	5	1.37	-12.70	670.48	**PSO**
MEA	MEASA	PUT	Jul-10	5	0.45	-11.20	123.80	**PSO**
ICO	ICORA.o	PUT	Jun-10	5	1.00	-11.95	388.05	**PSO**
ICO	ICOUA	PUT	Sep-10	5	1.35	-14.20	930.80	**PSO**
WATG	WQUSV	PUT	Jul-10	12.5	1.70	-11.95	668.05	**PSO**
WATG	WQUSV	PUT	Oct-10	7.5	1.05	-11.95	408.05	**PSO**
YZC	YZC	PUT	Jul-10	15	0.70	-12.70	337.30	**PSO**
SEED	QSW	PUT	Aug-10	7.5	0.90	-13.45	526.55	**PSO**
GE	GE	PUT	Sep-10	14	0.75	-13.45	436.55	**PSO**
AA	YJA	PUT	Oct-10	10	0.58	-12.70	277.30	**PSO**
AGU	VAVMI	PUT	Jan-11	45	3.10	-9.70	300.30	**PSO**
AOB	ZZDMA	PUT	Jan-11	5	1.65	-12.70	812.30	**PSO**
F	OKFMU	PUT	Jan-11	7.5	0.94	-15.70	830.30	**PSO**
XLU	ORUMB	PUT	Jan-11	28	1.78	-10.45	345.55	**PSO**
T	VFEME	PUT	Jan-11	22.5	1.84	-14.95	1457.05	**PSO**
PAY	XKXMB	PUT	Jan-11	10	1.40	-11.95	548.05	**PSO**
SLV	XUXMO.:	PUT	Jan-11	15	1.60	-10.45	309.55	**PSO**
ACH	LCF	PUT	Jan-12	20	3.50	-10.45	689.55	**PSO**
TOTALS:				15.55	1.42	-263.65	11378.53	

Even though I have $11378 in earned premiums - and I know I should be happy with that - these positions do pose a slight dilemma for me. The problem is this: since the puts are all cash secured, a large amount of money is "on hold" in my account(s) until these positions settle or expire. This is not a bad thing when you think of the premiums earned as an interest rate of about 7% per year. But I might also miss out on some good buying opportunities with all my money tied up in puts!

And here is a list of my closed positions as of the last revision of this book (only one of these options – SCHF – was exercised, meaning I had to purchase the stock:

STK	TYPE	PRICE-C	PRICE +/-	CLOSE	RETAIN	ROI%
AIG	CBO	0.25	38.89	15.30	0.00	0.00
AIG	CBO	0.16	1500.00	143.55	117.10	442.72
PAY	CBO	2.25	50.00	215.30	55.60	34.82
EROC	CSO	-0.85	-5.56	-94.70	-14.40	-17.93
VALE	CSO	-2.49	283.08	-508.45	-388.90	-325.30
VALE	PSO	-0.08	-91.01	-26.45	141.10	84.21
C	PSO	-0.16	-40.74	-176.45	77.10	30.41
GE	PSO	-0.01	-96.77	-17.70	124.60	87.56
SCHF	PSO	0.00	-100.00	0.00	669.55	100.00
VALE	CSO	-2.83	-0.35	-576.45	-18.90	-3.39
SLV	PSO	-0.23	-74.44	-56.45	113.10	66.71
VLO	CSO	0.00	-100.00	0.00	69.55	100.00
ICO	PSO	-1.11	5.71	-791.20	-70.40	-9.77
YZC	PSO	-1.00	17.65	-411.95	-83.90	-25.58
C	CSO	0.00	-100.00	0.00	133.55	100.00
CDII	CSO	0.00	-100.00	0.00	39.55	100.00
		-0.44	99.03	-2285.65	791.20	25.82
		-0.22	0.27	-2341.85	12113.53	62.66

Your immediate reaction upon seeing these results might be "this seems like a whole lot of work for a $12113.53 gain!" which is the amount under the "RETAIN" column. But I closed some of these options by "rolling them up" to a more distant expiration date and in many cases, a higher premium. So if you look at the very *bottom line* for all options the bottom of page 102, you see that as of this very moment in time I have actually retained $15906.08 in premiums alone – this in just my first 6 months, and I consider that big money indeed!

Analysis of Closed Positions

Now let's pause for a few moments to ponder the above closed positions and see if my reasoning and decisions on opening and closing them were sound or not.

AIG – My decision here was absolutely sound, since even though I took a loss on the first option, I made an overall profit on the two. I might have made a greater profit if I held the second call option a little longer, by who can argue with a 1500% gain!

PAY – I bought this call for $159.70 and sold it for $215.30, making a very nice $55.60 profit ($34.82%) so this deal was absolutely sound, and not bad for my second trade!

EROC – I bought this call for $80.30 and sold it for a $14.40 loss. The reason I sold it was because I believed that EROC, which was selling for $4.50 at this time, was rapidly heading for between $6 and $7 per share. At the time of this writing the stock had indeed risen to $6.50 per share, so while I lost $14.40 by buying back the option to close the position, I gained $150 in equity appreciation! This is the real magic of trading stock options: you have many more choices than you do with a buy and hold strategy or by trying to "time" the market.

VALE – Now these option trades are a little more complicated, but let's see how I did. I first sold a combination on VALE that included a CALL at $27.50 and a PUT at $22.50, netting me a premium of $287.10. Later I decided that I really liked this stock and that the $27.50 strike on the call was too low, so I sold the call for a $388 loss, but then sold another call on VALE with a strike of $35 for $557 – a $169 net gain. Later on I decided that even $35 was too low a strike, so I sold the Jan 10 call for $576 – an $18.90 net loss, and sold yet another call with a strike price of $40 for a $749 premium. Let's look at my VALE options this way:

SYMBOL	TRAN DATE	SHR_BUY	SHARE-$	INVESTED	SOLD	NOTE
VALE.2	2008/05/22	50	41.50	2075.00	0	
VALE.2	2009/06/24	50	17.75	887.50	0	
VALE.2	2009/08/04	100	21.00	2100.00	0	2.3% DIV
VALE.2	2009/09/28	0	119.55	0.00	119.55	CSO JAN 10 27.5 VALE RFPAYo.2
VALE.5	2009/10/09	0	167.55	0.00	167.55	PSO DEC 10 22.5 RIOXX (WRONG ACCOU
VALE.2	2009/11/11	0	508.45	508.45	0.00	CBC JAN 10 27.5 VALE RFPAY
VALE.2	2009/11/11	0	557.55	0.00	557.55	CSO JAN 11 35 VALE VOHAG (ROLLUP FR
VALE.5	2009/11/23	0	26.45	0.00	26.45	PBC DEC 09 22.5 VALE RIOXX closed to sel
VALE.2	2010/01/07	0	546.75	546.74	0	CBC JAN 11 35 VALE VOHAG (to sell JAN 1:
VALE.2	2010/01/07	0	749.55	0.00	749.55	CSO JAN 12 40 VALE YGJ
VALE.2	2010/03/08	0	669.54	0.00	669.54	PUT JAN 12 25 VALE

The above table shows all of my VALE stock and option trades. The stock trades show shares purchased. Those records without a number of shares purchased are option trades. Before I traded any options on VALE I owned 200 shares at an average price of $30.72 per share while the stock was trading at $19 per share – a significant $2344 loss. By selling puts and calls on the stock, I earned $1182 in premiums, and this cut my loss in half. Since then, the stock has appreciated to its current price of

$31.40 per share (as of March 16, 2010) and this gives me a total gain of $2288.75. This is a 37% gain annualized at 20.48%. Had I done nothing I would just be breaking even. Even better, if VALE rises to $40 before Jan 12 it *might* be called away from me, but at that time I will have gained $4080 or 66.42% annualized at $36.51%, and that isn't a bad return!

C – In the case of C (Citicorp) I bought back the put with a strike of $4 to close because I decided that I wouldn't be comfortable buying more C at $4 per share. Besides, I was able to retain 30.4% of my premium for a tidy little profit.

GE – Since I retained 87.56% of my original earned premium, I believe this transaction was completely sound. After closing this, I sold six more put contracts on GE with an expiration of September 2010, and a strike price of $14 for a nice premium of $436.55, this while GE was trading at about $17 per share. This means I must keep $8400 in my brokerage account in case I must purchase 600 shares of GE at $14.00 per share. If you think of the premium as an interest rate, however, then you will see that I am actually earning a simple interest rate of 5.20%, annualized at 9.34%. I seriously doubt that GE will fall to $14 in the next six months, but if it does I will be happy to buy it at that price because GE is also a dividend paying stock with an annual yield of 2.3% - not great, but better than most CD's!

SCHF – This is the Schwab International Equity Fund. I sold an ITM (In the Money) put with a strike price of 30 on this while it was trading at $26.55, earning a premium of $669.55. While I hoped this wouldn't be the case, the put was almost immediately assigned to me, so I purchased this ETF for an immediate loss of $27.40, but this is well within the normal 1% swing of ETF daily price swings, so I am happy with the trade.

SLV – My option trades with SLV (the Silver ETF) are absolutely sound. I made a 20.86% gain of my SLV shares (annualized at 8.7%) before getting out. I sold the $15 put because the strike was $5 per share less than my average purchase price. I bought the put back only to reduce my exposure and retain 66% of my premium. Note that I also sold another $15 put on SLV with the JAN 11 expiration for another nice $307 premium, the equivalent of a 10.32% simple interest rate annualized at 8.08%.

VLO – Do you see that 100% ROI? That means that this option "expired worthless" or out of the money to the buyer, meaning I simply got to keep 100% of the premium without having to buy or sell any stock! The same is true with the "C" call option and CDII call option at the bottom of the list. These are the kinds of deals you should always look for in options trading!

ICO – I closed this Mar 10 put on ICO with a strike of $5 for a loss of $70.40 in order to sell a Sept 10 put on ICO with a strike of $5. In doing so, I increased my total premiums earned from $720 to $860 – a nice gain in itself. The real reason for doing this, though, was to avoid buying more ICO at $5 per share at a time when it was selling for about $3.80.

The premium was large enough that I would be in the money either way, but I decided I wanted to add a little more time value to the option with the hope that the stock would rise, and the option would eventually expire worthless to the buyer.

YZC – Now, if any of my closed options illustrate irrational thinking, it is this one. I bought back this $17.5 put to close for a loss of $283 in order to sell a different put with the same expiration date but a $15 strike for a premium of $337.30. In other words, I threw away all but $54 dollars of a $328.05 premium to avoid buying YZC at $17.5 at a time when it was selling at $23.50 per share! I really wanted to buy the stock back, but my thinking was that if I could get it at $15 per share I would save $1000. What I failed to consider though was that to drop to $15, the stock would have to lose 36% and that was not likely to happen. Even falling to $17.50 was a long shot. So switching my options the way I did served no other purpose than to throw a good premium away.

If there is a lesson to be learned in all of this it is this: Know why you assume a position with any option, be it a put, call, spread, or otherwise. Once you have assumed that position, do not change it unless there is some very compelling reason to do so. Usually when I sell I put I do so because I decide that, having received a nice premium I would be happy to buy the stock at the put price. To throw that premium away as the stock approaches the strike price in the course of normal market swings is illogical in the absence of other compelling information. This is exactly how many traders suddenly find themselves in very deep waters. Had I not closed the YZC position (and thrown away that premium), and had the stock dropped to 17.50 and then the option assigned to me, I would still have been $319.10 ahead! This is why it is so critical to have a good spreadsheet model and to use it effectively to make these decisions. In the case of YZC I had the model, but I allowed my emotions to affect my decision, rather than trusting the numbers right in front of me.

Analysis of Open Positions

The next two pages show all of my open (and closed) option positions in a table that is much easier to reference than the smaller tables in this book, but it only shows opening figures, gains, and effective interest rates if the option simply expires.

OPEN OPTIONS

STK	SYMBOL	OPTION	EXPIRE	STRIKE	PRICE-O	COMM	OPEN	TYPE
WATG	WQUDV	CALL	Apr-10	12.5	-2.30	-9.70	-239.70	CBO
VLO	VHBAE	CALL	Jan-11	25	0.75	-10.45	139.55	CSO
C	C	CALL	Jan-12	7.5	0.33	-16.45	313.55	CSO
VALE	YGJ	CALL	Jan-12	40	3.80	-10.45	749.55	CSO
VALE	YGJ	PUT	Jan-12	25	3.40	-10.45	669.55	PSO
MEA	MEAPA.(	PUT	Apr-10	5	1.37	-12.70	670.48	PSO
MEA	MEASA	PUT	Jul-10	5	0.45	-11.20	123.80	PSO
ICO	ICORA.o	PUT	Jun-10	5	1.00	-11.95	388.05	PSO
ICO	ICOUA	PUT	Sep-10	5	1.35	-14.20	930.80	PSO
WATG	WQUSV	PUT	Jul-10	12.5	1.70	-11.95	668.05	PSO
WATG	WQUSV	PUT	Oct-10	7.5	1.05	-11.95	408.05	PSO
GSI	GSI	PUT	Sep-10	5	1.30	-11.95	509.25	PSO
YZC	YZC	PUT	Jul-10	15	0.70	-12.70	337.30	PSO
SEED	QSW	PUT	Aug-10	7.5	0.90	-13.45	526.55	PSO
GE	GE	PUT	Sep-10	14	0.75	-13.45	436.55	PSO
AA	YJA	PUT	Oct-10	10	0.58	-12.70	277.30	PSO
AGU	VAVMI	PUT	Jan-11	45	3.10	-9.70	300.30	PSO
AOB	ZZDMA	PUT	Jan-11	5	1.65	-12.70	812.30	PSO
F	OKFMU	PUT	Jan-11	7.5	0.94	-15.70	830.30	PSO
XLU	ORUMB	PUT	Jan-11	28	1.78	-10.45	345.55	PSO
T	VFEME	PUT	Jan-11	22.5	1.84	-14.95	1457.05	PSO
PAY	XKXMB	PUT	Jan-11	10	1.40	-11.95	548.05	PSO
SLV	XUXMO.:	PUT	Jan-11	15	1.60	-10.45	309.55	PSO
CB	CB	PUT	Jan-12	50	6.50	-9.70	640.30	PSO
ACH	LCF	PUT	Jan-12	20	3.50	-10.45	689.55	PSO
	TOTALS:			16.18	1.58	-301.75	12841.63	

CLOSED OPTIONS

STK	SYMBOL	OPTION	EXPIRE	STRIKE	PRICE-O	COMM	OPEN	TYPE
AIG	UZLKU.o	CALL	Jan-10	2	-0.18	-9.70	-27.70	CBO
AIG	UZLAZ.o	CALL	Jan-10	2.5	-0.01	-16.45	-26.45	CBO
PAY	PAYAC.0	CALL	Jan-10	15	-1.50	-9.70	-159.70	CBO
EROC	EAUDA.>	CALL	Apr-10	5	0.90	-9.70	80.30	CSO
VALE	RFPAY.o	CALL	Jan-10	27.5	0.65	-10.45	119.55	CSO
VALE	RIOXX.o	PUT	Dec-09	22.5	0.89	-10.45	167.55	PSO
C	CMW.X	PUT	Jan-10	4	0.27	-16.45	253.55	PSO
GE	GEWMV	PUT	Jan-10	12.5	0.31	-12.70	142.30	PSO
SCHF	OSFMF	PUT	Jan-10	30	3.40	-10.45	669.55	PSO
VALE	VOHAG	CALL	Jan-10	35	2.84	-10.45	557.55	CSO
SLV	SLVPO.X	PUT	Apr-10	15	0.90	-10.45	169.55	PSO
VLO	VLBAY.x	CALL	Jan-10	25	0.40	-10.45	69.55	CSO
ICO	ICOOA	PUT	Mar-10	5	1.05	-14.20	720.80	PSO
YZC	YZCSC	PUT	Jul-10	17.5	0.85	-11.95	328.05	PSO
C	CCH.o	CALL	Mar-10	8	0.15	-16.45	133.55	CSO
CDII	CDSCZ.>	CALL	Mar-10	2.5	0.25	-10.45	39.55	CSO
	TOTALS:			15.61	0.77	-163.55	3064.45	
	GRAND:			15.89	1.17	-465.30	15906.08	

EXEC $	TODAY $	$GAIN	%ROI	P-SHR	SIMP%	APY%	DAYS
0.00	0.00	(239.70)	(100.00)	(2.40)	(19.18)	(55.55)	126.00
0.00	0.00	139.55	100.00	0.70	2.79	2.81	362.00
0.00	0.00	313.55	100.00	0.31	4.18	2.28	670.00
0.00	0.00	749.55	100.00	3.75	9.37	4.60	744.00
0.00	0.00	669.55	100.00	3.35	13.39	7.15	684.00
0.00	0.00	670.48	100.00	1.34	26.82	50.98	192.00
0.00	0.00	123.80	100.00	0.41	8.25	16.37	184.00
2000.00	1792.00	171.10	44.09	0.43	8.56	13.01	240.00
3500.00	3136.00	557.85	59.93	0.80	15.94	24.24	240.00
5000.00	4268.00	(72.90)	(10.91)	(0.18)	(1.46)	(2.80)	190.00
0.00	0.00	408.05	100.00	1.02	13.60	21.22	234.00
2000.00	1600.00	100.30	19.70	0.25	5.02	11.03	166.00
0.00	0.00	337.30	100.00	0.67	4.50	8.83	186.00
0.00	0.00	526.55	100.00	0.88	11.70	25.73	166.00
0.00	0.00	436.55	100.00	0.73	5.20	9.34	203.00
0.00	0.00	277.30	100.00	0.55	5.55	8.69	233.00
0.00	0.00	300.30	100.00	3.00	6.67	6.38	382.00
2500.00	2065.00	368.35	45.35	0.74	14.73	11.59	464.00
0.00	0.00	830.30	100.00	0.92	12.30	11.20	401.00
0.00	0.00	345.55	100.00	1.73	6.17	6.17	365.00
0.00	0.00	1457.05	100.00	1.82	8.09	8.25	358.00
0.00	0.00	548.05	100.00	1.37	13.70	11.77	425.00
0.00	0.00	309.55	100.00	1.55	10.32	8.08	466.00
0.00	0.00	640.30	100.00	6.40	12.81	7.00	668.00
0.00	0.00	689.55	100.00	3.45	17.24	8.68	725.00
=========	=========	=========	=========	========	=========	=========	========
15000.00	12861.00	10657.88	82.99	1.02	6.33	6.37	362.96

EXEC $	TODAY $	$GAIN	%ROI	P-SHR	SIMP%	APY%	DAYS
0.00	0.00	(12.40)	(44.77)	(2.48)	(124.00)	(1257.22)	36.00
0.00	0.00	117.10	442.72	2.34	93.68	924.14	37.00
0.00	0.00	55.60	34.82	0.56	3.71	71.21	19.00
0.00	0.00	(14.40)	(17.93)	(0.14)	(2.88)	(175.20)	6.00
0.00	0.00	(388.90)	(325.30)	(1.94)	(7.07)	(58.66)	44.00
0.00	0.00	141.10	84.21	0.71	3.14	25.43	45.00
0.00	0.00	77.10	30.41	0.08	1.93	12.56	56.00
0.00	0.00	124.60	87.56	0.25	1.99	9.45	77.00
6000.00	5312.00	(27.40)	(4.09)	(0.14)	(0.46)	(166.68)	1.00
0.00	0.00	(18.90)	(3.39)	(0.09)	(0.27)	(1.73)	57.00
0.00	0.00	113.10	66.71	0.57	3.77	13.90	99.00
0.00	0.00	69.55	100.00	0.35	1.39	4.66	109.00
0.00	0.00	(70.40)	(9.77)	(0.10)	(2.01)	(7.06)	104.00
0.00	0.00	(283.90)	(86.54)	(0.71)	(4.06)	(98.69)	15.00
0.00	0.00	133.55	100.00	0.13	1.67	3.78	161.00
0.00	0.00	39.55	100.00	0.20	7.91	18.51	156.00
=========	=========	=========	=========	========	=========	=========	========
6000.00	5312.00	(118.15)	(3.86)	(0.03)	(0.17)	(0.08)	63.88
21000.00	18173.00	10539.73	66.26	0.50	3.14	5.37	213.42

The left side of the above table is self-explanatory, and we have discussed the column information at length. The right side of the table requires just a little more explanation, so le me address that here before I discuss my remaining open positions. The EXEC column shows how much I would pay for the stock if it were assigned to me at the strike price. The TODAY column shows how much the stock is actually worth at today's stock price. If there are numbers in these two columns then the option is "In the Money" and would probably be exercised, although it might still not be. So in the above table you can see that both ICO puts, the first WATG put, the GSI put as well as the AOB put are all "In the Money" and could very well be put to me. But you will also readily see that only in the case of WATG would I lose $72.90 on the transaction, and it you look below that you will see yet another WATG put where I actually gain $408.05, thereby regaining all of my "paper" loss and then some. The "ROI" column shows what percent of my original premium is retained. Since the very first WATG is a call the premium is a cash outlay and is displayed as a negative value. "P-SHR" is the amount earned or loss per share, "SIMP%" is the simple interest rate earned or lost on the transaction, and "APY%" is the annualized percentage rate. Finally, "DAYS" is the total number of days the option *might be held* in the case of open options, and the total number of days that the open was *actually held* the case of the closed options shown at bottom.

Looking at this table you can readily see the value of trading options. First of all, look at some of those interest rates! In the case of the MEA Apr 10 put I am earning a 26.82% rate for only 192 days, or 50.98% when annualized! And this one is safely out of the money and scheduled to expire in only about 3 weeks at the time of this writing.

You can see that I sold another CALL (JAN 12) on C for a nice $313 premium, but since C is on the move as of late this time I chose a higher $7.50 strike price. You can see that the simple interest rate on this deal is only 4.18% or 2.28% percent per year, and that I received 31 cents per share as my premium. But should the stock rise to $7.81 per share (and there is no doubt in my mind that it will eventually) then my current $200 *loss* on C will become a $3270, 62% or 31.88% annualized rate or return, and I can live with that!

Also, look at how I doubled on Vale. At the time of this writing Vale is at $30.47 - right in the middle of $24-$40 put call combination. Even though this is less than my average cost per share for the stock, I currently enjoy a very nice $2375 *gain* on this position, and will only earn more in the future no matter which way this stock moves. An extra benefit of writing a put call combination like this is that as the price of the stock moves one way, the cost of closing the opposite position decreases.

You can see that I "doubled up" on both MEA and ICO selling puts with identical strike prices but different expiration dates. Here I am simply going for the maximum premium that I can earn. Currently I do not own either of these stocks, but I did in the past and I made nice profits on them, so I wouldn't mind buying them back if I could get them at less than my last selling price. If you subtract the "P-SHR" amount from the right hand page of the above table from the $5 strike price this will show the price I would pay for shares put to me. In all four cases, it is well below my last exit price on these stocks.

WATG is a special case. First, I purchased the APR 10 CALL with a strike of $12.50 at a cost of $239.70. "Wonder Auto" is a Chinese automobile parts supplier and I expect them to rise just as spectacularly as GEELY Auto has (I have not to this point mentioned GEELY Auto, but do a Google on them and you will understand what I mean). But right after I bought this CALL the stock took a big drop, and I doubt that it will rise above $12.50 before expiration. I still believe it is going to rise big time, though, so I sold these two puts *simply to finance the call I previously purchased.* Since I earned $530 on the puts my call was free, and I pocketed an additional $260 to boot! Of course, I could have bought WATG at today's price of $10.70 per share, but when you add the "P-SHR" amounts on WATG you see these puts give me a $1.32 without immediate risk.

GSI, a large Chinese steel company that should perform in China's growing economy caught my eye and my wallet to the tune $800 for 200 shares of stock at $4.04 per share. You can see that I sold four SEP 10 PUT contracts on GSI with a $5 strike price; since the stock is selling below $5 this is an ITM (In the Money) option, meaning the stock could be put to me at any time. So why would I sell an in the money put? Well first of all I have conviction that this stock will rise rapidly. And if you look at the above table you will see that if the stock were put to me today (when the price is right at $4.00 per share) I would still have a $100.30 profit, or .25 cents per share! I was very happy to buy the stock at $4, but by selling the puts I was able to really purchase it for $3.75 per share!

Actually, the one share that I fear being put to me the most is AOB, but even there I am earning 14.75% for holding that position, and if it is put to me today I will still be ahead more that $368 on the deal!

And take a look at CB (The Chubb Corporation). This is an expensive gem that I would love to own, but I didn't want to pay market, so by selling this put I pocket an immediate $640 premium, meaning I have already earned a $6.40 per share profit! The bottom line is that if the option were to be exercised today, I would still be $10,539.73 ahead of the game!

I have already discussed YZC, and how I lost most of my previously earned premium when I "rolled up" this position so let's move on the SEED. This is a huge Chinese agricultural company that produces – you guessed it – grains. By now you know that I am partial, at this point in time, to investing in big Chinese companies when the "option" presents itself to me. So when I read that this company should see 15% annual gains over the next few years I decided to test the waters. So I sold an out of the money put with a strike price of $7.50 at a time when the stock was selling for $10.20, earning a $525 premium, and this represents an 11.7% return annualized at 25.73%. And if this stock should *ever* drop to $7.50, I would gladly snatch it up because my actual cost would then be only $2.25 per share!

With GE (which I previously owned but sold at a 25% profit) I am again going purely for the premium and effective interest rate of 5.2% annualized at 9.34%, with the added hope that I might buy the stock back at less than what I previously sold it for, which was $16.25 per share at the time. So with the stock selling at $16.50 per share, I sold this SEP 10 put with a strike price of $14 to make a very nice $436 premium! While I seriously doubt that GE will drop back below 14 (indeed, today the stock is trading at $18.60) I would be very happy to have it "put" to me at $14 given that the stock also pays dividends!

The rationale behind my AA position is almost identical to my rationale for the GE position. While I no longer owned this stock I would be happy to buy it back at less than what I sold for previously, especially if I could earn a good rate of return on the money that would be put "on hold" while I waited for that magical price. So when the stock was selling at $13.78 per share I sold this far out of the money PUT with a $10 strike for a nice $277 premium, which is a 5.55% return annualized at 8.69%. This at a time when Schwab's money market is paying less than .005%!

AGU is in this same boat: I no longer own this great stock but I believe in it so thoroughly that I was almost tempted to buy it back at its current price of $71.33 per share! The main reason I didn't is because this agricultural commodity stock (potash) is highly volatile, and its current price is $13 over my last selling price of $58. I know I got out too early, but this is a roller coaster. I originally purchased it at $70 per share and I had traded this equity many, many time before I was finally able to get out of it with a decent 11% (5% annual) return. But here is was, once again over $71 per share. So selling this put with a strike price of *only* $45 was icing on the cake. There is very little chance of the option being exercised, and this was a relatively short term commitment (9 months) to earn a 5.55% rate annualized at 8.69%.

Check out "F" (Ford). Who could resist selling a put on Ford with a strike price of $7.5 at a time when the stock was selling for $14 per share and all the analysts were saying that the stock could only going to go higher? Yes, I could have laid out $1400 to buy 100 shares, but it seemed more logical to me to *sell* 9 put contracts on Ford with a strike price of $7.50 for a really grand $830 immediate gain (which is 12.30% annualized at 11.30%), and virtually zero percent chance of a loss! Having done that, I could now buy 50 shares of Ford for $700 and keep the remaining $130 for spare change!

XLU is a big utilities sector ETF. My forward thinking strategy is to write put options against option-able exchange traded funds rather than individual stocks in order to achieve a greater degree of diversification. So I sold this put to lower the price that I would pay for XLU should it be put to me. In the meantime I am earning 6.17% on the money I have put aside to purchase XLU should the option be exercised.

I sold the JAN II put on T (AT&T) for similar reasons. AT&T is a dividend paying stock, and at 6.7% the highest of the DOW, so I would be happy owning it. When I sold this put with a strike price of $22 the stock was selling for $25.50. I earned a premium of $1457.05, or an 8.25% annualized rate of return by selling this option, and I am quite glad I did!

I previously discussed PAY (Verifone), and that was a call option that I *purchased* for $159.70 and was actually able to sell later for a $55 profit. What was amazing about that was that it was only my second options trade, and most calls expire worthless! What I didn't tell you is that I previously owned the stock as well, and I eventually sold it for a profit of $1,200.00 or 12.6% annualized at 7.7%. I got out of the stock because the company had some "accounting issues." Since then the issues have been resolved and the stock has been on a roll. So I sold this JAN 11 PUT with a strike of $10 at a time when the shares were trading at $13.75. In the process I made a $548 premium, or $13.70% annualized at 11.77%. At the time of this writing the stock is trading at $20.19. Had I bought the stock outright I would have done only slightly better, but I would have taken a $1375 risk instead of pocketing a sure $548 gain!

I previously discussed my reasons for taken my position with SLV (The silver trust) so I won't discuss it in detail here, other than to say "look at those returns!"

Rounding out this discussion is ACH (Aluminum Corp of China), another stock that I wish I had never sold, and would be happy to buy back. I previously made $2661 in profits, or 5.5% annualized. Selling this put with a $20 strike while the stock is $25 gave me an additional $689 annualized at 8.86%.

Now, About My Losses…

It is now July, 2011 and eight months have passed since I last updated you my returns. If you have been reading the newspapers then you know that a whole lot has happened in that eight months. Our economic recovery has not been nearly as rapid or dramatic as the optimists predicted it would be six months ago. In fact, the U.S. economy has stalled on a number of fronts. Home prices are *still* falling, and foreclosures are *still* rising! Consequently, most consumers are *still* tightening their belts, spending less, doing nothing to spur the economy. For a while gasoline went back above $4.00 per gallon, and this in turn forced prices on almost everything to rise, although the government still refuses to utter the word *inflation.*

The global economy is a real mess, too. Greece, Spain, Portugal and Italy are all teetering on bankruptcy, and this is putting tremendous fiscal pressure on the European economy as a whole. The Chinese are implementing various measures to cool down their red-hot economy, and this has forced down Chinese stock prices in general, and this is especially so among the auto companies. Back in November the Chinese automobile industry was on fire and stocks were skyrocketing across the board. My favorite auto stock – Geely – was trading as high as $5 per share, but then the Government placed restrictions on the number of new cars that could be sold in China's biggest cities, and this caused automobile stocks in general to tumble. Of course, this downward momentum was further spurred by other Chinese measures implemented to slow down their ever-increasing rate of inflation.

Alarmingly, there was also an explosion of revelations showing that stock fraud was rampant in a certain class of Chinese stock involving reverse-mergers (several of which I owned) and this caused investors to flee many of these Chinese stocks, even the legitimate ones.

So lets take a look now at a new snapshot of my option-traded stocks taken on this day, July 19th, 2011 to see where I stand today. I must first warn you, this looks really ugly: much uglier than it really is, and I will explain this as we move along. But first let's just examine the numbers, and only those for stocks that I leveraged in one way or another with options.

The table on the following page displays those numbers. The first column shows the stock symbols. Where the stock symbol is followed by a number, that number represents an account number. When the symbol is followed by an "*" the totals shown represent all activity for the stock in all accounts. "Price" is the last trading price for the stock; GAIN is total gain or loss; %GAIN is the percent gained or lost; YRLY% is an annualized rate of return; SHR is gain or loss per share; HELD is gain or loss of shares held, and REALIZED is gain or loss of shares sold. You will see #DIV/0 in columns where no shares were purchased; those gains are option trades only.

	PRICE	GAIN-$	%GAIN	YRLY%	SHR	HELD	REALIZED
	1.12	20900.37	11.00	6.44	1.08	(6423.55)	27323.92
AIG.*	27.72	238.59	43.04	302.10	11.93	0.00	238.59
AOB.20	1.13	(4052.10)	(68.80)	(16.48)	(4.27)	(4052.10)	0.00
ACH.*	19.90	2661.77	39.87	28.26	8.87	0.00	2661.77
AGU.*	90.61	2200.09	9.94	4.01	5.37	0.00	2200.09
C.20	37.66	147.47	1.53	0.47	0.13	13.34	134.13
CAAS.20	8.41	(2939.20)	(32.20)	(19.82)	(4.90)	(2939.20)	0.00
CB.*	61.23	640.29	#DIV/0!	#DIV/0!	0.00	0.00	640.29
CDII.*	0.99	55.65	18.55	16.39	0.28	0.00	55.65
EROC.*	11.14	189.78	39.48	53.97	1.86	0.00	189.78
FBP.20	4.51	(187.84)	(18.97)	(17.44)	(3.03)	(187.84)	0.00
LEGYF.20	0.27	347.55	34.37	11.01	0.12	164.63	182.92
VALE.20	32.71	2670.12	43.65	13.82	13.35	2670.12	0.00
WATG.*	5.42	(4806.20)	(30.06)	(18.72)	(3.20)	(4806.20)	0.00
XLU.40	33.17	2149.26	19.48	13.27	5.60	2149.26	0.00
AA.50	15.34	979.58	97.04	38.67	9.52	27.46	952.12
AIB.50	1.64	(323.81)	(64.76)	(59.54)	(8.10)	(323.81)	0.00
CCME.50	1.55	(1677.95)	(53.73)	(89.97)	(16.78)	(1677.95)	0.00
F.*	12.94	7208.80	49.72	14.01	2.12	1645.60	5563.20
GE.50	18.47	1485.35	37.77	17.34	4.91	12.21	1473.14
GLD.*	155.70	1369.90	12.21	6.00	9.45	0.00	1369.90
GSI.50	1.52	(1657.54)	(43.53)	(29.64)	(1.66)	(1657.54)	0.00
ICO.*	0.00	2254.72	21.99	11.30	1.13	0.00	2254.72
MEA.*	5.80	895.58	19.26	6.54	1.12	0.00	895.58
PAY.*	43.43	1210.95	12.60	7.77	1.73	0.00	1210.95
REMX.50	24.79	626.07	27.35	48.00	6.26	626.07	0.00
SEED.*	4.20	1172.62	#DIV/0!	#DIV/0!	0.00	0.00	1172.62
SCHF.50	28.32	333.54	5.56	3.62	1.67	333.54	0.00
SCEI.50	2.33	(1032.55)	(28.00)	(16.70)	(2.58)	0.00	(1032.55)
SLV.*	39.08	2527.65	22.29	6.65	4.72	0.00	2527.65
T.*	30.06	1457.05	#DIV/0!	#DIV/0!	0.00	0.00	1457.05
TC.50	9.92	(419.17)	(11.64)	(21.14)	(1.40)	(419.17)	0.00
YZC.*	38.09	3414.90	52.28	36.77	8.54	0.00	3414.90
VLO.50	25.42	1998.04	43.19	17.36	9.97	1998.04	0.00
TOTALS	23.93	20900.37	11.00	6.44	1.08	(6423.55)	27323.92

Okay – have you recovered your composure? Good! There's quite a bit of red, but let me explain why it is not as bad as it looks on paper. First and foremost, the reason it is not as bad as it looks is because these *are on paper*, and are for the most part, *paper losses.* It looks like a loss, but these are not *realized losses.* In fact, I only have one *realized loss* out of the bunch, and that is the SCEI loss of $1035.55. This is a real loss because I sold out my position for less than I paid for it, locking in the loss. The other "losses" are on paper only; I still own these stocks and they may – and probably *will* – go back up in value. Stocks do after all, go up and down all the time. So if you look at the bottom line in the REALIZED column you will see that *I have actually locked in a realized gain* of $27,323.92 on this group of stocks, and that ain't bad!

If you look at the very first column containing the stock symbols (AOB, C, CAAS, etc.) you will see that eight of them are highlighted in red. These are all Chinese stocks and as I stated in the introductory paragraph to this section, Chinese stocks as a class have been beaten down severely over the last 6 months due to a number of factors, including reports of fraud. Three of these were attacked by short sellers, dramatically forcing their prices down: CCME, SCEI, and WATG. It turned out that CCME severely overstated their earnings. The stock was de-listed from NASDAQ where it had traded at $22 per share, and re-listed on the PINK sheets where it now trades at $1.55. Now, if I had purchased CCME stock outright (and I *would have* had I not started trading in options) then I would have taken a position with 600 shares for a total investment of $7,100 (about $11.83 per share). From this purchase price point the stock dropped almost 90% when it went to the PINK sheets, so had I bought the stock outright my loss would have been $6,400 instead of the $1,677 paper loss that I record now. So while I may not have made the best stock pick, I certainly did the right thing by taking a position with options rather than purchasing the stock directly. On a final note on this company, I should reiterate that this is a legitimate company with a real business. They have paid their dues for overstating their earnings. Hopefully things will only go up from here, allowing my to erase this paper loss over time. But in any case, I cannot lose more than the $1677.95 shown in the HELD column.

WATG (Wonder Auto) is an automotive original equipment supplier of components, and they have gained some notoriety of being chronically late at filing their required forms with the Securities Exchange Commission. So once again they missed their deadline, but this time significantly so NASDAQ halted trades of these shares, freezing them at $5.42 until the issue is resolved. Immediately shorts went after WATG, and numerous legal firms filed class action lawsuits against the company. So my position with this stock is really up in the air. But it could get much, much worse. I took a very aggressive position with this stock, and currently hold 1500 shares with a total risk of $12,936 (I earned $3090 from options trades; had I not done this, my risk would be $15,989). So if this company does get de-listed or if the claims of fraud show any sign of merit then my real loss could be substantial. It won't wipe me out, because I have made other gains in the market that will provide a nice cushion against this potential loss, but it will still hurt. Nobody likes to find themself staring down the barrel of a possible $15,000 loss! On the other hand, if the company is vindicated then I might see the stock price soar dramatically. It's a roller coaster, but once again, no pain, no gain!

The third Chinese stock in this group, SCEI, was also severely attacked, especially by one short seller known as "Alfred Little." However, unlike most of the other companies charged with fraud, SCEI launched a spirited defense and even filed a lawsuit of its own against Alfred Little. Still, I feared this growing bubble of fraud in Chinese stocks so I made an emotional decision to sell my SCEI stock at a real loss of $1032.56, but my loss was cushioned by $488 by the sale of a Sept PUT option on SCEI with a strike of $2.50. In the last month SCEI stock has charged back from $1.20 to $2.33, so my PUT option may work out very well in my favor!

CAAS, another Chinese automotive component original equipment manufacturer also took a severe beating in this fraud mania, but the company is legitimate and the stock price is on the rise again. In fact, the whole class of Chinese small caps is now considered a bargain market utopia, and stock gains have been substantial over the last month. So a good play for me at this point in time might be to sell, say, four Feb 12 PUT contracts on CAAS with a strike price of $7.50 at a premium of $2.70, for an immediate net gain of $1068. This would cut my paper loss by 1/3, and would give me 2.89% on the money that I would place on hold to purchase this stock if it were to be assigned to me. If the stock were not assigned to me within the 215 days remaining, I would earn 4.91% APY and tremendous upside potential for my total return. If the stock is assigned to me I would purchase it for $7.25 per share and this would reduce my average price per share from around $15.21 to about $12 per share, and that would suit me just fine!

So the bottom line is that while I *do have* some big losses – both realized and paper losses – I also have some very big gains. While I am holding a $6423 paper loss, I have a $27,000 realized gain, with almost half of that being from option premiums. I made some very risky, even horrible stock picks, but by using options I reduced my risk considerably and managed to make a healthy profit, and that's the bottom line!

Some Do's, Don'ts, and Future Strategies

Here are just a few of the things I plan to do in the future to lower my overall risks and increase my overall profits:

Brokerage Account

Do not execute a lot of trades, as the tax rate is quite high for short term gains. Of course, I don't want to miss out on any good opportunities to make a good profit when such present themselves, but be I must always be fully cognizant of the tax reporting requirements and consequences before each trade.

Sell PUTS to purchase some good stocks, funds, or diversified ETF's that pay a good dividend. If the option is assigned to me I will want to hold it for the long term to avoid short term gains if possible. To increase my earnings on the stock in the interim I will set up a straddle by selling both a far out of the money PUT and a far out of the money CALL with a target annualized rate of return of better than 10%. The idea would be to sell options that would likely expire worthless, and only against equities that I would be happy to own if assigned against me.

Roth IRA

I believe I can be a little more aggressive and speculative in my Roth IRA than I should be in either my traditional IRA or standard brokerage account. Since the Roth in not taxed at withdrawal, my investment goals in this account should be prioritized as 1) Capital preservation, 2) Speculation, and 2) Capital appreciation. Toward that end I will look to purchase stocks or funds representing stocks with solid balance sheets and cash flows but higher than average growth potential; i.e., small caps and small cap ETF's. I will either buy shares directly or sell puts to buy them on a pullback. I will sell straddles on any that I own once I have reached a target gain of 15% with the idea of increasing the gain to at least 20%.

Traditional IRA

The traditional IRA account is taxes as regular income at withdrawal. While I do want to earn as much as possible in this account, my goal priorities here are 1) Capital Preservation, and 2) Capital Appreciation. Invest only in large cap AAA stocks, funds, and ETF's. I want to maximize my use of out of the money covered calls on any stocks that have already realized a significant gain.

And now for those Do's and Don'ts:

DON'T put a stop-limit order on a stock for which you have written a call option. The reason is that the stock could take a sudden but momentary dip during which your shares would be sold. But the stock price could then bounce back substantially, leaving you the seller of a naked call, and your potential losses would be unlimited!

DO sell covered far out of the money calls on any stock that you have realized a substantial gain on, and if you really, really like the stock, sell an out of the money put as well, striving for a double digit return on the put.

DON'T close your short puts to "roll up" to a later expiration date unless you have some compelling reason to do so. Doing so will only surrender a good portion of the nice premium that you previously pocketed.

DO roll up your short puts, or close the position completely if you decide that you really DO NOT want to own this stock! Never sell puts on an equity you do not really want to own!

DON'T buy puts or calls unless you are certain of the direction the stock will move; long positions usually expire worthless!

If you **MUST** sell options without owning the underlying stock, **DO** make sure you are covered either in CASH or by the other leg of a SPREAD. If you write a call that obligates you to deliver stock, you can cover yourself by purchasing a call that allows you to buy it (usually at a higher strike price, for protection). Don't get caught with your pants down in a naked put or call, because your potential losses will be unlimited!

DO know what your entry, exit, and break even points are on every trade. Even with all the preparation I did to ensure that I was fully cognizant of these points, I still managed to make some mistakes, most notably in the case of YZC in which I gave up almost all of a well-earned premium for no appreciable gain in potential earnings.

DON'T engage in spreads until you are very comfortable with your knowledge and skills. Spreads are wonderful for limiting your potential losses, but they also lower your potential gains by virtue of the additional premium you will pay to open the position. If you are convinced that a stock is good one, why bet against it? Instead, either purchase the stock outright, or write out of the money puts for lower interest rates of return, or in the money puts for a higher rate of return 9and greater chance that you will actually purchase the shares. And always, always sell covered calls whenever your stock has substantial gains!

Summary of Strategies Discussed in this Book

Call Bought to Open You purchase a call option that gives you the right - but not the obligation - to purchase shares at a specific strike price on or before the expiration date.

Put Bought to Open You purchase a put option that gives you the right - but not the obligation - to sell shares at a specific strike price on or before the expiration date.

Covered Call You own a long position in stock and you sell a call option that gives the buyer the right to purchase your stock at a higher strike price on or before the expiration date.

Cash Secured Put Sold to Open You sell a put option giving the buyer the right to sell you shares at a specific strike price on or before the expiration date, and you have cash in your account on hold in the event the purchase is assigned to you.

Combination A combination is both an out of the money put and an out of the money call – both with the same expiration date - purchased on an underlying stock with the expectation that the stock will not make a dramatic move in either direction. The goal of the combination is to earn additional profit on premiums when the market is moving sideways.

Bull Put Spread   You anticipate that the price of a given stock is going to rise, and you hope to profit on this trend by taking cash premiums in lieu of purchasing the stock directly. You sell a number of puts to open, and you purchase an identical number of puts to open, but at a lower strike price, and this leaves you with a credit as shown:

ACCT	CNTS	STK	SYMBOL	OPTION	EXPIRE	STRIKE	PRICE-O	COMM	OPEN	TYPE
2	10 C	C		PUT	Jan-12	2.5	0.50	-16.45	483.55	PSO
2	10 C	C		PUT	Jan-12	1	-0.08	-16.45	-96.45	PBO
						1.75		Credit:	387.10	

The maximum gain in a bull put credit spread is the premium earned, while the maximum loss is the difference between the two strike prices minus the premium earned. In the example given above, the maximum loss is 1130 as shown below.

EXE	OPEN	CLOSE	GROWTH	EXEC $	TODAY $	$GAIN
Y	3.27	**0.00**	(100.00)	2500.00	0.10	(2025.30)
Y	3.27	**0.00**	(100.00)	1000.00	0.10	894.50
						(1130.80)

Had the stock alone been purchased at $2.50 per share the maximum loss would have been $2,500. The bull put spread works well for those who want to profit on the potential rise in a stock's value without purchasing the stock up front. Yet the gains are limited, and the potential for loss is very real. Still, this strategy can be less risky and less costly than purchasing the underlying stock outright.

Bear Call Spread   This strategy is often used when a stock is expected to decline in value. Assume XYZ stock sells for $100 per share, a call option with a strike of $100 for goes for $2 and a call option with a strike of $95 goes for $5. To implement a bear call spread, you would buy the $100 call option for $200, and sell the $95 call option for $500 for a quick profit of $300.

If the stock price drops below $95 at the expiration date then neither option will be exercised, and your profit is secured. But if the stock price rises above $100 (say to $105), then both options will be exercised. The call you purchased would be worth $500, but since you paid $200 for it your gain would be $300. And the call you sold lost $1,000 in value, but since you previously pocketed $500 your loss is only $500. Subtract this from your $300 gain, and your total loss is $200. Here is how the bear spread described above looks, excluding commissions:

STK	SYMBOL	OPTION	EXPIRE	STRIKE	PRICE-O	COMM	OPEN	TYPE
C	C	CALL	Jan-12	100	-2.00	0.00	-200.00	CBO
C	C	CALL	Jan-12	95	5.00	0.00	500.00	CSO
				97.5		Credit:	300.00	

EXE	OPEN	CLOSE	GROWTH	EXEC $	TODAY $	$GAIN
Y	100.00	**105.00**	5.00	10000.00	10500.00	300.00
Y	100.00	**105.00**	5.00	9500.00	10500.00	(500.00)
						(200.00)

This strategy works well for the bearish investor who wants to make profit on declining stock. In this example his maximum loss would be $200, no matter how high the stock price might rise!

Additional Resources:

If you do a Google Search for "Resources for Option Traders" you will receive in excess of 18,000,000 hits. This is just on the lists you are likely to find.

My advice to those who wish to learn how to trade options is to do your research well. All of the material you need is out there, and most of it is free, so don't get caught up into spending a lot of money on proprietary learning programs when you are just starting out. Perhaps the best source of information on the list is the Options Industry Council

Characteristics and Ricks of Standardized Options
This is the guide that every trader must acknowledge they have read and understand before they can begin trading options. You can request a copy from your broker, or directly from the Options Clearing Corporation.

The Options Clearing Corporation (OCC)
http://www.theocc.com/

The Options Clearing Corporation is the world's largest derivatives clearing organization.

Chicago Board Options Exchange
http://www.cboe.com/
Exchange market on which many of the top options are traded.

Options Industry Council
http://www.888options.com/
One of the best sources for free information on trading options.

optionsXpress
http://www.optionsxpress.com/
An online options broker (Be sure to check your own for info!).

Investopedia
http://www.investopedia.com/
A great online guide for options information.

E*Trade
http://www.etrade.com/
Another online brokerage for stocks and options.

Zecco
http://www.zecco.com/
Still another online brokerage. Can also use to trade options.

Optionetics
http://www.optionetics.com/
Offers proprietary option tracking and trading tools. Most of their software requires a fee.

Investools
http://www.investools.com/
This company offers investor training courses.

CNBC
http://www.cnbc.com/
Don't forget the big media companies as a great source of timely information!

CNNMoney.com
http://money.cnn.com/
Another great site for investor information

American Stock Exchange
http://www.amex.com/

Dow Jones
http://www.dowjones.com/
Business and financial news site.

Carl Allen Schoner

Jan 29, 2010

Hi Dad,

I executed a trade today that I thought I would interest you.

This is how it worked out. I had $18,000 sitting in my Schwab savings account earning .05%. I then discovered that AT&T stock was paying a 6.7% dividend, and I decided that I should get a piece of that action.

The stock was selling today at $25.50 per share. I wouldn't mind owning it at that price, but I preferred to get it at a big discount. So I sold 8 PUT options on this stock with a strike price of $22.50. This means that between now and Jan, 2011 I *might* have to buy 800 shares of AT&T at $22.50 per share ($18,000). So I must leave my $18,000 on hold in the Schwab account to purchase the shares should they be sold to me. In the meantime, I immediately earned $1457.05 for selling the PUTS, and this is an 8.77% annualized rate of return on my $18,000!

If the price of the stock goes up the price of my puts will go down, and it is conceivable that in 6 months I might be able to eliminate my obligation to buy this stock by buying back the PUT options for perhaps pennies on the dollar, which means I could get out for the cost of commission alone (in this case the commission is $14.95). I have done this many times already. Getting out early will also have the effect of dramatically increasing my annualized rate of return!

If on the other hand the stock price should drop and I have to buy it at $22.50 (won't happen unless the price drops below that price) then I will really pay only $20.68 per share (because of the $1457 premium I earned) and I will then own an asset paying me a hefty 6.7% in dividends – much better than the .05% savings rate!

This is just one of the strategies I use to get a bigger return while maintaining a conservative position! I wish I could tell you everything you need to know in order to get started in options, but right now – I've got to get back to trading!

Carl

About the Author

Carl Allen Schoner holds a degree in behavioral science and is a certified clinical hypnotherapist and seminar speaker. He is also an experienced investor and writer with much experience in the areas of stocks, bonds, options, insurance, and annuities. As a gifted artist and author his articles and illustrations have appeared in many prestigious publications such as Consulting Magazine, The California Law School Journal, Chess Life Magazine, and The Saturday Evening Post.

Notes

www.ingramcontent.com/pod-product-compliance
Lightning Source LLC
Chambersburg PA
CBHW022003170526
45157CB00003B/1116